Other *Yale Daily News* Guides from Kaplan Books

Yale Daily News *Guide to Fellowships and Grants*
Yale Daily News *Guide to Internships*
Yale Daily News *Guide to Succeeding in College*

Other Kaplan Books to Help You Prepare for Your Future

Résumé Builder & Career Counselor
Reality 101
Student's Guide to On-Campus Job Recruitment
Going Indie: Self-Employment, Freelance, & Temping Opportunities
The Buck Starts Here: The Beginner's Guide to Smart Financial Choices

OLDEST COLLEGE DAILY   FOUNDED JANUARY 28, 1878

Working Knowledge

150 Successful Professionals Tell You How to Use College to Get the Job You Want

By Julia Kahr
and the staff of the *Yale Daily News*

Simon & Schuster

Kaplan Books
Published by Kaplan Educational Centers and Simon & Schuster
1230 Avenue of the Americas
New York, NY 10020

For bulk sales to schools, colleges, and universities, please contact Vice President of Special Sales, Simon & Schuster Special Markets, 1633 Broadway, 8th Floor, New York, NY 10019.

Project Editors: Cynthia Brantley-Johnson and Richard Christiano
Production Editor: Maude Spekes
Cover Design: Cheung Tai
Desktop Publishing Manager: Michael Shevlin
Managing Editor: David Chipps
Executive Editor: Del Franz

Special thanks are extended to Judi Knott and Linda Volpano.

Manufactured in the United States of America
Published simultaneously in Canada

January 1999
10 9 8 7 6 5 4 3 2 1

Library of Congress Cataloging-in-Publication data is available
ISBN: 0-684-85239-X

Table of Contents

Many books feature career advice for college grads.

What makes this book different?

1. The advice in this book doesn't come from just one expert . . . in fact, it comes from 150. College graduates on all steps of the career ladder—from entry-level positions right up to the CEO's office—were interviewed for this book, and their advice reflects both the pitfalls they've endured and the successes they enjoyed so far. They've already been to the places your career trajectory will take you, and they'll tell you what you can do now to pave the way for future success.

2. The professionals interviewed have made the mistakes, so that you won't have to. This is not a fawning tribute to 150 success stories . . . the graduates interviewed for this book not only tell you what went right for them, but also what went wrong. If you want to know what people in your chosen field of work would have done differently in college, turn the page and read on.

3. You can start implementing the advice in this book right now, while you're still in school. Most career guides deal exclusively with on-the-job strategies, leaving the college student without any information on how to get started. This book is a valuable guide to the classes, extracurriculars, and other activities you need to prepare for the world of work.

About the Author

Julia Kahr, a native of San Francisco, graduated from Yale University summa cum laude in 1998. She was publisher of the *Yale Daily News* in 1996–97. In college, she completed internships at McKinsey & Co., Merrill Lynch, the Advisory Board, Shearman & Sterling, and Banque National de Paris. She is currently employed in the New York office of the Boston Consulting Group.

Acknowledgments

My purpose in writing this book is to make available to others the information and tools that I and my friends lacked. To gather this information I had to ask for help. This book is primarily the product of the experience, expertise, and generosity of those whom I interviewed.

I have also benefited greatly from the guidance and suggestions of my publishers and editors. This project was first presented to Maureen McMahon of Simon and Schuster, who has been consistent and steadfast in her interest and support. I am indebted to Cynthia Brantley-Johnson for the initial editing of the manuscript, and for many helpful and incisive contributions that I believe have rendered the book both more useful and more readable. The help of Jessica Jewell, my colleague as publisher of the *Yale Daily News*, was invaluable in getting the project moving.

My parents deserve particular acknowledgment for their help and confidence in me throughout the project. Finally, I thank Michael Donofrio for his unfaltering love and support.

OLDEST COLLEGE DAILY   FOUNDED JANUARY 28, 1878

Founded on January 28, 1878, the *Yale Daily News* is the oldest college daily paper in the United States. The all-student staff publishes a 10- to 16-page newspaper five nights a week, reporting stories related to the Yale and New Haven communities. Financially independent from the university, the *Yale Daily News* supports its own production through student-sold advertising.

Boasting an alumni list that includes Henry Luce, Sargent Shriver, Potter Stewart, William F. Buckley Jr., Garry Trudeau, Calvin Trillin, and Shelley Fisher Fishkin, the *Yale Daily News* has been called the best unofficial undergraduate school of journalism. Today's *Yale Daily News* remains committed to the mission of teaching journalism, conducting skills workshops, and hosting alumni speakers.

In addition to the daily newspaper, the *Yale Daily News* publishes a weekly news magazine, a monthly compilation of stories, and the *Insider's Guide to the Colleges*—a guidebook to the nation's colleges created by interviewing current undergraduates.

Most recently, the *Yale Daily News* has entered a joint venture with Kaplan Books and Simon & Schuster to produce a series of guide books to assist and advise students throughout their college careers. Titles include the *Yale Daily News Guide to Succeeding in College*, the *Yale Daily News Guide to Fellowships*, the *Yale Daily News Guide to Internships*, and this publication. Authored by staff members of the *Yale Daily News*, all the books offer valuable tips for college success drawn from the experiences of actual students.

Introduction

Welcome to a book that will give you specific and practical help in entering your career, through the words and experiences of those who preceded you as college students and graduates. These people range from recent alumni who have found great jobs to corporate recruiters and heads of major corporations.

When you finish college or university, you will need a job. This book will help you make the choices during your college years that give you the widest possible choice of the best possible jobs, whether or not you continue your studies after college. Your decisions about your studies, about your extracurricular activities, and about the work you do during the summer or the school term can make getting a good job easier or harder. It's possible to luck into a good job, but much safer and more comfortable to qualify for it.

How do you figure out what you should do—about your classes, your jobs, and your activities? What is it that can make a big difference to your employability? In which cases is it worth working harder or forgoing what you would like the best right now, in the confidence that this will pay off in the not-too-distant future?

You can answer these questions on the basis of your own experience, but that experience is limited. You can talk to friends, parents, experts, but each of them has experience that is focused on a particular region or field. This book mobilizes a much wider range of experience. The goal is to let you see what others have done in college and after college, and how it has worked out for them. Then you can draw your own conclusions and see how this experience applies to you.

The purpose is not to make you worry about your future. Rather, it's to spare you worries that you can easily avoid.

Over 150 interviews were conducted with college graduates to assemble the experience base for this book. Some of the people interviewed are recent graduates with keen memories of what worked and what failed for them during the job hunting process. Many others are managers or human resources professionals who are actively involved in recruiting college students.

The occupational range is wide, from high tech to retailing, from farming to dentistry. College background of the people interviewed is also very diverse, extending to all areas of the country and ranging from large, state universities to small, junior colleges to engineering schools and Ivies.

The words of these interviewees are distilled and summarized in this book. Where conclusions are stated, they represent a strong majority view of those who contributed their knowledge, rather than a personal conviction of the author. Where contrasting views emerged from the interviews, fair expression was given to each.

The goal is to be as much help to as many students as possible. If you're studying Aeronautical Engineering at Cal Tech or MIT and getting a 4.0

average, then maybe you're all set. If you're less sure of what you want and where you're headed, and if you have doubts about how you can get a job that is right for you, then this book is for you.

You will learn from people who have succeeded—and most of them frankly admit that they have succeeded despite some setbacks and mistakes. Many have exciting jobs. Some run major labs, others have extensive marketing responsibilities, and quite a few have been able to start their own businesses. Some run big companies. These people will show you how it's possible to move from a fulfilling and happy college experience to a fine first job and a solid career.

In order to encourage absolute candor, each interviewee was offered the opportunity to remain anonymous or have some part of their identity— name, age, and/or university or institutional affiliation—disguised. Many are identified only by the school they graduated from. This assured that both good and bad experiences could be discussed candidly, and many accepted the offer of anonymity.

This book was written because it's needed. No other book draws on the advice and experience of hundreds of college graduates and focuses on helping you work towards your future. Their stories are intriguing, gripping, and informative. Their advice is sincere and thoughtful.

So consider this your invitation. Learn from what others like you have done, draw your own conclusions, and make your own choices with confidence.

How Will You Find a Job After Graduation?

1

When you've been a student for 16 years, the cycle of school years seems to go on forever. How can it ever end? What on Earth will happen after it ends? Something very different.

Get Ready for Something Very Different

What will happen is not much like anything else you've ever lived through. It's different from summer jobs and after-school jobs. The most basic way in which a real job is different is that unlike a school year or college, or your whole education, jobs don't come to a natural end. You can get fired, find another job, or—unimaginable as it may seem right now—retire. But one way or the other, you're going to be working for more than 40 years . . . twice as long as you'e lived up to now.

> *I just finished my first week of work. Every day, you go in at 8:30 and I leave at 5:00. I've done that kind of thing before, but only*

for a little while. I don't think I'll like doing this for the rest of my
life. I'm used to being much freer. This is depressing.

—Harry, age 21

Why It Matters

Most likely, from graduation onward you're going to spend more hours
working than doing anything else—including sleeping. That's more time
than you have ever spent in classes. At least in terms of sheer hours, work
will be the most important thing you do.

> Unless you prepare yourself to qualify for a good choice of jobs,
> you may find that you have to work at times and in places that
> seriously conflict with other priorities that are very important to
> you, including family and recreation.

Work will be your most important activity in another way, too. While a few
people can afford to work without being paid, you're probably not one of
them. So, your work will be essential because it's the only way you can avoid
having to ask for handouts from your family and friends. Mooching is
pretty unpleasant, and it can't go on indefinitely.

Your job also affects your housing, your car, your vacations, and your
comfort. Your job will largely determine whether your days are spent
happily or miserably, whether you're optimistic or terrified about your
future, and whether you're self-confident and pleased with yourself or
disappointed and defensive.

That can be frightening to think about, which could be why so many of us avoid thinking about it for so long. Sometimes we're even told not to think about what happens after college.

> *At orientation, the dean spoke. I was too excited to listen for long, but he said a liberal education didn't prepare you for any particular job. He said not to worry about jobs. Now I wish I hadn't listened to even those first few sentences before tuning out!*
>
> *—Barry, age 25*

Waiting until graduation to think about a job won't doom you to perpetual unemployment. If it did, half of last year's graduating class would be jobless, and they aren't—less than 10 percent have remained unemployed. What happened to the others between graduation and employment has many variations, but it's often something like this:

> *My parents gave me a nice trip as a graduation present. On my way back from Japan, I kind of ran out of money in San Francisco. A temp agency put me in this small company. Later they offered me a regular job, so I took it. I liked San Francisco better than Minnesota. The work was interesting, but I was never really trained for anything. I got promoted, but when the company merged I discovered I didn't have any transferable skills. Come to think of it, I never had any reason to do that kind of work. I'd rather work with people than with numbers.*
>
> *—Jessica, age 28*

Landing On Your Feet . . . In the Wrong Place

Jessica landed on her feet, as most of us do. But the spot where she landed probably wasn't the place she would have chosen.

Working is no game, but you can think of the job market as a game board. As a student, you're not on the board. When you get a job, it puts you on the board . . . somewhere. Where you start on the board, and whether you're a highly prized piece or a humble pawn, depends on you—what you are and what you have done. Your initial place on the board determines where your next move can take you. If you're a pawn, you can move only straight ahead . . . which means you can be blocked easily. If you start in a better position, you'll have a wider choice of moves.

What to Do if You Just Don't Know

Sam, a sophomore, says happily that he has no idea what he will do after he graduates. He has lots of interests and abilities. His Dad was that way and it worked out just fine for him, so he's not worried. "Other than getting good grades," said Sam, "there's nothing I can do to improve my chances of getting what I want—since I don't even know what I want." Sam studies pretty hard because he takes pride in his accomplishments. For all the rest, he merely does what interests him.

Since he doesn't yet know what kind of work he wants, Sam could instead be focusing on making himself attractive to a broad range of employers. Then, when job offers come in, he can expect to have a number of diverse choices. This is necessary if he is to have any hope of choosing a job that fits his preferences when those preferences finally emerge. Otherwise, Sam could end up having to choose from a very sparse and unappealing set of job alternatives. And one way or another, Sam will end up working. He's neither lazy nor a deadbeat.

If you press him in a friendly way, Sam will tell you, "Well, if I have to wait for a while to find the right job, that's okay. My parents are in a position to help me. And if my first job works out badly, I have plenty of years ahead of me to get on the right track."

Though he jokes about the joy of being free from job-getting worries, Sam knows much more about the job he wants to do than he's willing to let on. For instance, if you gave him a long list of occupations or jobs, he could immediately eliminate most of them without any soul searching.

It's not surprising that Sam doesn't want to be a farmer or a miner. But his range of interests is actually much narrower in ways that are not immediately obvious. Talking to him, you could see that Sam would not be happy in any job where he had to do selling, or where he had to work directly with the public, either face-to-face or by telephone.

In fact, once you got him into the spirit of the thing, Sam could probably work his way down any list of possible jobs and eventually eliminate every last one of them, for one reason or another. That is part of what his "I have no idea" means. He has no idea of a job that would satisfy him. And that may feel like a good way to avoid both thought and any sense of pressure— for a while.

It makes no difference whether you're undecided because there are 20 different jobs you would love to do, or whether you're undecided because every single job possibility seems detestable. Either way, you will find it advantageous to evaluate and prioritize, rank the possibilities in order of preference, and work from the top down. Sam would place the sales jobs at the bottom, for example.

For Sam, the job possibilities are not likely to get much more attractive between now and graduation. This being so, Sam will be much better off distinguishing the less bad from the worse and targeting the less bad right now, no matter how much this process distresses him.

Eventually, Sam will get around to learning things that make him more interested in certain jobs. If he leaves this learning to the last minute, then at best he can use it only in choosing among offers—of which he's not likely to get very many. But if he begins thinking and learning about work sooner—even right now—then he will be able to do a great many things to improve his chances of getting a job that will please him, and he can adjust his target as he goes along with some time to spare. It's not fatal to take a job you aren't happy with or even to get no job offers right after graduation, but they are setbacks that are well worth avoiding.

A Job Is for Keeps

To prepare yourself for the right job, you need first of all to be sure you understand what a permanent job is. Maybe you think you already know—after all, you must have had some summer jobs. Trouble is, a regular, permanent job is as different from a summer job as a long-term, live-in relationship is different from a hometown summer romance. A summer or term-time job, like a summer romance, has a natural ending point. A regular job doesn't, and neither does a live-in relationship.

I had always worked during term-time and in the summer. I just paid attention and used common sense, and my bosses liked it fine. When I graduated, I was lucky to get an interesting job in a hazardous waste facility. It was as different from my student jobs as night and day. I never knew I could get so tired, and the responsibilities were serious. I'm too busy to think of going anywhere else.

—David, age 25

Actually, David might not have been working any harder in the waste facility than he had earlier, at a copy shop and in a restaurant. But the level of stress was higher. In a part-time job or a summer job, even if you need them and they need you, it's often enough to just carry out the day-to-day routine. You don't have to worry about being pushed out or about pushing your way up.

In many regular jobs, however, you have to figure that you're probably headed either up or out. When you look to your left and to your right, you will see young people in the jobs like yours, not oldsters. The people who used to have those jobs didn't die or find the fountain of youth. Some were promoted, a few were fired, and others left for a better job somewhere else.

Your Job and Your Boss

The person who decides whether you go up or out is the same person who probably made the decision to offer you a job in the first place: your boss. He or she will very quickly become a very, very important person in your life. It's like going back to first grade, where the teacher loomed very large indeed. Whether she smiled or frowned at you made it a good or a bad day. It's exactly the same way with the boss, unfortunately.

At college and even in high school, you were much less dependent on any one person. You might have five or eight teachers during the course of a year. Each gave you a grade, independent of the others. But at work, as in first grade, there will be just one person who decides what your job is, and who later decides whether you have done it well: the boss. As a practical matter, his or her judgment—even if imperfect or dead wrong—is unlikely to be questioned.

> When you get a job, it will not only put you in a line of work, such as customer service or sales, but also in a company, and in an industry, all of which will determine your exact position on the game board. Getting that first job will also put you under a particular boss. Which boss may be as important as which line of work and which company or industry.

Of course, you could not choose your first grade teacher, and you can't "hire your boss" either . . . right?

Wrong. If you have any choice of job or if you can get more than one offer, then you have a choice of boss. You won't want to take a job without knowing your prospective boss. And if you're sensible, you won't accept a job if you have any serious doubts about the boss.

I interviewed in several accounting departments. In my interview with Jane, I didn't sense any particular rapport, or interest in me as a person. but it was my only real job offer. Within a month, I learned that no woman working for Jane had ever survived. Within a year, I was gone. It was very unpleasant.

—Caroline, age 23

Like so many others, Caroline simply wanted a job. And she got a job . . . for a while. But she had no *choice* of job, since she managed to obtain only one offer or accepted the first offer she received. You might say she's fortunate in one respect: She won't have to regret making the wrong choice, since she didn't have a choice. Most likely, if she had had any choice at all, she would not have chosen to accept the offer from Jane, with whom she felt no affinity. Caroline wound up in a bad job either because she hadn't managed to make herself more appealing to employers and bosses, because she hadn't made a broad enough job search, or because she ended it too soon.

The Goal: Widest Possible Choice

In some ways, getting a job is similar to a process you have already successfully completed; namely, the process of getting into college. You wind up at one college, just as you wind up with one job. But on the way, you applied to a bunch of colleges. Since colleges choose their students according to differing criteria, you wanted to have more than one way to win, or at least to avoid losing. Thus, you were advised to make a number of applications, and that was good advice.

You probably know someone who didn't take that advice. He had his heart set on one college and bent all his efforts on getting into that one. Maybe he reluctantly filed a couple of "safety" applications at colleges he felt sure of getting into but didn't particularly care about. When his first choice didn't come through, he was left with alternatives he found unappealing.

And then there were probably some other people you know who had a different problem. Although they were aware they would be going to college, they just were not much turned on by any particular college. So, they simply didn't bother doing the kinds of things that would have improved their chances of getting admitted. These people also wound up displeased and dissatisfied.

It can be the same way with jobs. You shouldn't focus entirely on one dream job because the dream may come to an end. Make yourself an appealing candidate for a range of jobs that you know enough about to be confident that they can be appealing to you. Then, with the benefit of your final college experiences, including the job interviewing, you can pick the one that suits you best.

Your Hour in the Sun

As a college senior, you have a unique opportunity to be sought after by employers. It's only at that time (unless you later go to professional school) that prospective employers will actually come to you, via your college placement office. You won't have to mail off dozens or hundreds of letters to companies that turn out to be "not hiring now," or that won't even bother to reply. As a senior, you can be courted, even wined and dined, rather than having to traipse around to employment offices, hat in hand and ready for long waits, put-offs and put-downs.

To take full advantage of this special opportunity, start now. Learn about jobs and employers. Sketch your target zone. Locate the bull's-eye within that zone. This will enable you to focus your attention and economize your effort.

If you have no idea right now as to whether you most want to receive offers from Proctor & Gamble, American Airlines, or a congressional office in Washington, then you need to give attention and energy to satisfying the requirements of *all* of them—as well as dozens of other employers. You will have more to do, and you're likely to have less complete information about how to do it. But if you pay attention to the hiring criteria and requirements of none of these employers, then you're likely to get offers from none of them. After all, at a typical college placement office a popular employer may get over a hundred applications for every student that it will ultimately hire. How can you be that one successful applicant if your efforts to stand out and be chosen do not begin until the last minute? Remember:

> The less you know about what you want to do after college, the more effort you'll need to make in order to get a good choice of jobs.

There is much less effort, and less risk, in thinking and exploring to learn more about who you are and where you want to go, than in trying to make yourself a credible candidate for every imaginable job.

How You Can Win

To get onto the game board of work, you have to play a few essential warmup rounds while you're still in school. You can regard these rounds as each involving a choice that you make, followed by a result—typically a choice that is made by someone else. For instance, you choose a course, and decide how hard to work at it. Then the professor chooses your grade. He may also choose what kind of recommendation and job-hunting help, if any, to give you. (It might help you to know that in some fields and at some schools, employers pay professors substantial "consulting fees" to steer the right students in their direction. So your relationships with some teachers might be more important than they seem, and you might get some help from teachers that is not entirely motivated by a desire to help you.)

Similarly, you pick part-time or summer jobs. These can reward you with pay and experience. They can also render you more (or less) employable in particular jobs. You try out for a team, and you may end up a star, or more likely a humble intramural player. Each of these warmup rounds feeds into subsequent ones, just as one friendship can open the way to another.

The payoff from all this comes when you go out to find a job, and it comes in the form of job offers. As we have seen, the more good offers you get, the better off you are. If the employer you like best doesn't offer you the highest pay, then perhaps you can get him to improve his offer on the strength of other offers you have received. Ultimately, you will accept employment.

> *I wanted to be a buyer for Affiliated in New York, but they offered Chicago. Fortunately, I also had an offer from Federated in New York, and that gave me the leverage to get Affiliated to take me in New York. I'm very happy with Affiliated, and I remain friendly with Federated. That's my ace in the hole.*
>
> *—Peter, age 24*

Peter's experience shows how the other interviews and even the job offers you don't accept can be of value to you later. These successful efforts widen your choice of jobs and enable you to improve the best offer. They can also expand the scope of your possible later moves by providing contacts and possibilities that continue to have value after you start work.

The wider the choices that you open for yourself, the better the outcome will be, both in getting your first job and later. Some of the things you can do during your years in college can make you more attractive to a wide range of prospective employers, both immediately and later. These are the opportunities that are most worth pursuing because they can pay off even if you change your mind later about your job targets. Only 21 percent of the college graduates interviewed for this book felt that they had gotten as many job offers as they would have liked.

The Process

Start with an overview of the job-hunting process. We have seen that getting a job is in some ways like getting into college. First, you decide where you want to apply. Where you want to apply should actually have some influence on what you do for quite a while before you start preparing your application. Of course, your ideas about where to apply may change, and your program and activities may need to be adjusted accordingly.

For jobs, even more than for colleges, it's important to ensure that when you apply, you do so in such a way as to assure the most favorable possible attention to your application. Family, friends, or other people can put you in direct contact with your prospective employer. This can help a great deal.

Once you have applied, both colleges and potential employers consider your *file*, the documents you have provided. This file often includes a transcript. If they become interested in you, prospective employers then subject you to procedures aimed at evaluating you in comparison with other candidates—for instance, interviews. You interact with the employer, generally over a period of weeks. The third phase is the employers' decision-making process, leading to your being accepted by one or preferably by more of them. Lastly, you make your own choice, accepting just one employer.

Although the decision of exactly where to apply doesn't have to be made until the winter before you graduate, you benefit from picking your targets much sooner. Intel and Sears are not looking for the same college graduate any more than MIT and Claremont are looking for the same high school graduate. Although they are, on the whole, looking for quite different people, the various colleges' admissions procedures are nevertheless quite similar. The same goes for employers like Intel and Sears.

Now look in more detail at the key steps that can lead to a job offer. The explanation below shows that this process can stop short of your getting an offer in any of several ways. First, something you have done must lead to a decision to interview you. Normally, what immediately triggers the interview is the employer's review of the résumé (otherwise known as a *CV*, for *curriculum vitae*) you have sent together with a letter introducing yourself and expressing interest in the position (called a *cover letter*). You might have also sent other documents, such as transcripts and recommendations. All together, these pieces of paper constitute your file, to which other documents, such as interview reports and correspondence, will later be added.

You won't have access to the file on you that is maintained by your employer. Nonetheless, you will need to make a continuing effort to ensure that this file includes everything about you that you want the employer to consider. Yet the file must be concise and compelling, rather than diffuse and diluted by documents that have only marginal impact.

> The company's decision to interview you is a key positive step in the hiring process. In fact, up to that point your efforts should be expended not on getting hired, but simply on getting interviewed.

The initial interview or interviews may include your seeing two or more people, most often one-on-one but sometimes together. Normally, this round will include only one or at most two company people, whose task is to "screen" you to see if you qualify for more extensive consideration. These representatives will also screen a number of other applicants, possibly a very large number. The function of this part of the process is to choose some of the candidates initially interviewed for further consideration.

The first interview results simply in a decision either to eliminate you, or else to proceed with additional interviewing. Hence the first interviewer or interviewers have the opportunity to reject you, but not to hire you. Your task is simply to survive the screening and move on. If you do survive, you will be interviewed again by different people. There may well be a third set of interviews before the decision to make you an offer can finally be reached. Between these interview phases, an attempt may be made to check your references or to verify claims you have made in your résumé.

Finally, after it makes an offer, the company may press you to make a decision rapidly. Their main motive for this is to keep you from seeking other offers that might be better than theirs. They may also be open to negotiating some of the terms of their offer in order to induce you to sign quickly.

Who Decides?

Getting an offer, for instance an offer of admission into a college or a fraternity, may seem like a process that is deliberately kept mysterious. A faceless bunch of people sit around a table, and they reach a decision by shouting, voting, or debate. You wind up with a decision for which no one is really responsible.

Actually, life is sometimes much simpler than it seems, even in universities. A former dean of admissions at Harvard was renowned for taking a whole stack of applicant files home with him each night during the busy season. He would come back in the morning with each file marked *admit* or *reject*. Not only that, but he was able to comment in detail on each evening's television shows. He was a simple man, and he kept things simple. So much for the admissions committee.

Maybe colleges don't work that way any more, but when it comes to companies, the image of collective decision making on hiring is almost totally unreal. There is most often only one person who can make the decision to give you an offer: the person you're going to be working for, your prospective boss. It wasn't always that way, but that is how the process tends to work now.

You may wonder why these decisions are not left to "professionals," the corporate equivalent of a Dean of Admissions, perhaps someone working in a Personnel or Human Resources department. Well, think of it like this. Suppose your mother and your father both have cars that they use to get to work, and that your mother's car is about to be replaced. Who will make the final decision about what car to buy for her to drive? Will it be your father? Or will it be some expert they hire? Neither is likely. Your mother will make the final decision herself because she's the one who will live with the results of the decision. Similarly, if you had a younger brother or sister about to go to college, you would be very reluctant to tell him or her plainly and simply what college to pick. You won't get much credit if you're right, and what a mess it will be if you're wrong!

That is also how hiring works. The boss will be responsible for the performance, the value, and indeed the fate of the person who is hired. Everyone else is glad to let her choose that person herself—with whatever advice she wants. She will choose a person she's confident of working with effectively to get the results she needs. And she's very unlikely to think that grades, teams, or societies are enough to determine that. She will want to look you in the eye and hear what you have to say.

But before you ever get to see the boss, and probably before she ever gets to see your file, other people are likely to be involved in deciding whether you should be interviewed, and in determining the results of the first interviews. These people may include human resources types. They are likely to have criteria and preferences that differ considerably from the boss's. There is more than one hurdle for you to surmount.

Among the other decision makers are likely to be people who have had only one or two years experience at the company. If the company recruits at your campus, they will often be people who went to your college. Such people are thought to be the most likely to establish rapport with you, to assess what you and your file have to say, and to communicate relevantly and effectively their enthusiasm about their jobs, so that you will be motivated to want to work with them.

Companies, unlike some educational institutions, don't tend to make decisions democratically by voting or by committee deliberation. Individuals will make a series of eliminative decisions about you during the hiring process. In the early stages, some of these decisions may be made quite mechanically, but by the time you get to the end of the pipeline subjective judgment will prevail. The challenge is how to muster your efforts so as to drive this process towards the decision you want, a job offer.

> By the time you actually apply for the job, there will be a lot of facts about your experience and qualifications that you can no longer change. But if you start now, you can make yourself a much stronger candidate for good jobs. Consider how what you do can affect each step in the process, from application to job offer.

Getting Invited for an Interview

No company has time to interview everyone who seeks employment, and some don't have time even to interview all Harvard honors graduates who want employment. Furthermore, all but the tiniest companies receive large numbers of résumés from people whom it would obviously be a waste of time to interview because their interests and qualifications don't match the company's needs. Somehow, they've got to sift through the pile and find the few that will get a positive response: an invitation to be interviewed.

My office gets an average of over a dozen résumés per day, depending on the time of year. Managers are invited to funnel the résumés they receive directly in to me, but they don't have to do so. On an average day, my assistant would reject all of the résumés except a couple, which he would pass on to me. We have some rough rules of thumb. For instance, we're not interested in anyone who isn't in the top half of his class.

—*John, age 32*

John's assistant has plenty of other things to do besides glance at résumés. When he looks at a résumé, he can't see the person, only the words he has written. So, what do you think this anonymous assistant is going to do?

Is he going to make a highly scientific and precisely reasoned choice, even if it takes several hours to do so? Is he going to figure out which candidate will best fit the needs of each boss who is trying to make a hire? None of the above. Most of the résumés will end up as waste paper, so he will treat them all accordingly. He will try to satisfy John's criteria with as little effort as possible. The assistant doesn't want John asking "Why on earth did you give me this one?" But he doesn't have to worry about being blamed for throwing a résumé away, or for marking it to receive a polite "We will keep you on file" letter. In fact, no one, not even John, is likely to know who made these negative decisions or on what basis.

In order for you even to get an interview, your résumé must impress a busy person who is in a great hurry and has many other things to do, such as John's assistant. In a way, writing a résumé is like writing an advertisement: You can't expect anyone to read every word of it. They'll glance at it quickly, the way they glance at all ads. If the first glance doesn't ignite a spark of interest, then the page is turned and the opportunity is lost. But this is not a book about how to write a résumé: There are already plenty of those. This is a book about how to make yourself appealing and salable, so that your accomplishments and promise can't fail to hit the reader in the eye, even if your "advertising" is not the product of a top Madison Avenue firm. A mediocre advertisement for a great product is more effective than a great one for a mediocre product.

There is another way. Your résumé won't have to leap out of a big stack if it's given individual attention and interest by a manager. This will happen if you already know that manager, or if his attention is called to your candidacy by someone else whom he knows or respects. The manager generally doesn't care about who you know, but he relies upon some of the people he knows. If, while you're in college, you make yourself favorably known to some of these people, then your résumé can fly over the obstacles to the interview like a well-designed paper airplane.

Getting the Job

The final decision to make you a job offer will result primarily from your interviews, although you need a good résumé to get to the interviewing state.

> *I'd say evaluation of the candidate was based 30 percent on the résumé and 70 percent on the interaction I had with the candidate.*

—*Eric Zausner, former partner, Booz, Allen & Hamilton*

There are two reasons why interviews have the heaviest weight in the hiring decision. First, your success in almost any job will be critically dependent on your effectiveness in oral communication with co-workers, managers, and perhaps outsiders such as customers. An interview provides direct evidence of your oral effectiveness that no document ever really can.

Second, managers' decisions, like your own, are based primarily on the most recent evidence. That is human nature. By the time you've had a couple of interviews, your résumé is nearly forgotten. Or at least, it has been reinterpreted and reevaluated on the basis of the additional detail and explanations that you have provided.

There are, of course, interviewing skills just as there are résumé-writing skills. But what matters most are not any specific skills, but rather who you are when you finish college and have your employment interviews. Who you are will be the sum of your experiences, insights, and accomplishments. If you're the same person you were at high school graduation, you won't be a very good candidate for employment unless you want to work bagging groceries or babysitting. This book will help you use your remaining college years to become a more effective and able person, so that you can project these qualities strongly, both in what you write and in what you say in an interview.

Who Are You?

When you set your job targets—kind of work, industries, companies—your targets will be personal and unique. They will reflect what you like to do and the goals that you set. In setting those goals, don't sell yourself short. Few, if any, heads of major corporations graduated as top students of the most selective colleges. A far larger number were never voted "most likely to succeed" and went to colleges that are less elite. This is not to say that you should aspire to be a big boss, but merely that you shouldn't give up on what you want to do because you feel that others are smarter or better positioned.

Most people get the most enjoyment and satisfaction out of doing the things they do the best. So, for example, if you find that you're clumsier than others at working with your hands, then chances are you won't like the kind of lab work that is dependent on manual dexterity. You find out what you like to do and are good at by trying different things and making an effort to learn how to do them well.

The kinds of things you do at work are a lot different from most of what happens at school. At work, there are few if any textbooks or tests. But there's a tremendous diversity of job tasks available, most of which have little in common with studying. So, you may find that you're a lot better at some kinds of work than you were at being a student, and that you like and succeed at the right kind of work much better than you like and succeed at studying. The surest way to find out how well different jobs suit you is by trying them as early as possible.

Finding Work You Like

If you have a strong interest, or have found something you love to do, then push ahead in your thoughts, inquiries, and actions to see how this interest can frame your career. Here are just a few stories from the many interviewees who turned their interests into satisfying jobs:

> *I learned to fly in high school. It's what I like to do best. There aren't many commercial pilots who are women, but with the encouragement of my family, I got the technical training and practical experience I needed to be competitive while in college. Now I fly for the commuter affiliate of a big airline.*
>
> *—Kathi, Occidental College, age 29*

Not all passions start as hobbies. For some students, a compelling interest is sensed within the college setting itself, though not necessarily in classes.

> *All I really cared about in school was athletics, and by the time I got to college I was thinking about how to stay with sports, though I didn't have the talent to be a pro. Now I'm a college director of athletics, doing what I have always loved to do. I'm lucky.*
>
> *—Gordon, age 45*

Some would say that for Gordon, it was more a case of being smart than of being lucky. He knew what he liked, and he had the brains and the courage to translate that into career terms, and aim his education accordingly. Others in Gordon's situation might have made the mistake of concluding that sports are just for kids, and looked for something else to do.

Many college activities in addition to sports can expose you to challenges and skills that extrapolate into careers.

> *I loved music, but I wasn't satisfied with my playing. So, I became manager of the college orchestra. We went on tours, I met people, and I now help to administer a major professional orchestra. This is the work that I'm cut out to do.*

> *—Arnold, age 27*

If you're good at an academic subject, you can find areas of overlap or application where it qualifies you for careers outside the university.

> *I was always good at math, but found it very dry. In college I discovered a course on applying math to business decisions. The professor became my mentor and I wound up as a specialist in litigation analysis, running my own small firm.*

> *—Arthur, age 33*

Do not wait for graduation day to seek out a bridge between courses and work. What you learn in the work setting can feed back to make your studies far more relevant and valuable.

My interest is in international relations, and in my internships with foreign policy organizations, I found there was a shortage of Middle Eastern specialists. I turned my course work in that direction.

—Peter, age 23

Think about which applications of the fields you like to study will give you the job content you want.

Psychology is the discipline that fascinates me, but I want to spend my time helping basically healthy people become more productive. A professor helped me get a summer job at a firm that counsels management teams. I never imagined there could be such fulfilling work!

—Andrea, age 24

When your imagination and your contacts with professors fail to strike a spark, your college's career counseling service may have something worthwhile to say.

I wasn't quite sure what I wanted to do during my first two years of college. In the spring of my sophomore year, I went to the career office and asked for some advice. I told them that I was an intellectual history and French double major and that I liked writing, coming up with creative ideas, and people. They suggested I try an internship in advertising. I did and have been working in advertising ever since.

—Abby Wittenberg, age 25

Sounds like an inspired suggestion by the career office. In fact, it's a suggestion that merits a further look. The appropriateness of advertising as a field for Abby was obviously based upon "I liked writing, coming up with creative ideas, and people." That is a description of advertising! The suggestion was in no evident way based upon Abby's being an intellectual history and French double major.

Often, there's no clear link between your course preferences or major on one hand, and your most likely career interest on the other. The alignment goes deeper, to your basic preferences for activities, no matter what their subject: talking with people, writing, or coming up with ideas. That is what added up to advertising for Abby.

Of course, Abby might not have liked the answer she got at the career office, in which case she was entirely free to ignore it. Or, she might have tried advertising and hated it. Evidently she thrives on it, but that is no proof that she would not have been twice as happy and fulfilled doing something or other else. Still, she was almost surely better off trying an internship in advertising rather than spending her remaining two college years taking interesting courses, working random jobs, and waiting for enlightenment as to her occupational destiny. You are better off with a hypothesis to test than you are with a blank screen.

> If you start early, and you're aggressive in seeking job and internship opportunities both during the term and in the summer, then you have an excellent chance of finding work that you like to do and want to do.

Maybe in two years or in twenty years you'll move on. Your needs can change, and the market will change, too. Nevertheless, next year, this year, right now, you'll be better off with a hunch, a concept, a hypothesis to test, rather than a total blank. You'll be better off setting your course towards a light, however dim, rather than drifting.

The strongest feedback comes from a well-chosen job or internship. Sometimes a job you find rather humdrum and unrewarding can position you to move towards more attractive possibilities. Frederick's story, below, illustrates this point:

> *As a scholarship student, I was given a low-paying dining hall job, but I got into the organization side of it. This led me to seek out a better job in a local hotel banquet department. I found I liked selling banquet and meeting services. Now, I'm a student at the Cornell School of Hotel Administration.*
>
> *—Frederick, age 24*

Try It, You May Like It: Sales

Maybe your interests seem mild rather than passionate, leaving you with no clear focal point for testing concrete job possibilities. Nevertheless, your preferences are probably not as flat as you imagine. Most likely there are some job tasks that you would dislike and avoid. Perhaps up to now you have not had to think much about them, or you have managed to avoid them. You need to survey these dislikes and decide whether they are deep-seated and lasting, or whether they should be challenged by practical experience.

Take selling, for example. Some jobs involve directly convincing someone to buy something. That is what stockbrokers have to do, as do IBM sales representatives and travel agents. There are people who thrive on selling, and they love to do it.

> *When I got a waitressing job, I made sure it was at a restaurant where I really liked the food—that's common sense. I was enthusiastic and the customers grooved on that. Later I sold clothing—same idea. I loved making women really happy with their clothes. Now I'm in a job where I have to train other salesmen and turn them on. It's great!*
>
> —Marisa, age 26

Selling involves getting others to do things, and it can be very satisfying, as well as financially rewarding. But possibly you have tried it, hated it, and are sure that you would never want to do it again. In a bygone era, many students got summer jobs in door-to-door sales. Some loved it and went into a wide range of sales careers. Others found that they were not suited to sales.

These days, it's more likely that you have never actually tried selling, though you may have strong negative feelings about it. If you're interested in people and like to talk to them, if you're somewhat forward rather than shy, then seek out an opportunity to try selling. You have nothing to lose and a great deal to gain.

> *To hear my parents talk, salesmen were the scum of the earth. And the idea of my becoming one! In my freshman year, a laundry offered commissions for signing other students up. It sounds humdrum, but I enjoyed it. I set my own hours and got paid for results. I was hooked.*
>
> —Martin, age 24

Martin's goal is not to reach retirement as a star salesman, or even as a sales manager. Selling skills can help you rise in management, all the way to the top. They can help you get backing to start your own business, and they can contribute enormously to the success of that business. If you can sell customers, then you can probably sell your superiors on your ideas, and sell investors as well.

> If you can't stand selling, then you need to turn your career focus towards activities where selling is relatively unimportant.

Some such specialties include operations, controllership, and engineering within large organizations. You might also aim at an industry or type of organization where sales is a less crucial function. These include industries with commodity-type products and companies that are exposed to only limited competitive pressures, such as some utilities and many governmental and nonprofit organizations.

I liked the idea of having professional skills rather than having to compete head to head. But at law school I saw that nowadays practicing law involves constant selling. So, I accepted a job with the Department of Housing and Urban Development. The work is interesting, and I feel I'm doing some good.

—*Thomas, age 29*

Do You Enjoy Working with Other People?

Some jobs are relatively solitary, but most are not. This is a big difference between school and work. At school, you study primarily on your own. You take tests and are graded individually. Your contacts with the professors, your "bosses," tend to be formal. Your time communicating with fellow students is largely social—just fooling around rather than work. Even a lot of the apparent teamwork outside the classroom is really something else. You can be a star tennis player or wrestler, or even captain of a team, without having to worry much about working with others.

Working a job is altogether different when the job is full-time and permanent. Even if you're an architect or veterinarian or physician practicing by yourself—an arrangement that is less and less common— you're going to have to work with others, whether they are draftsmen, nurses, assistants, or billing agencies. If you're not a solo practitioner, your contribution will be entirely merged with and subject to performance by your co-workers, and by people above and below you in the organization.

> I would come up with these clever process improvements and they'd work fine in the lab. Take them into the plant, and they'd fail every time. It was like throwing a message over a wall. Anyone there?

> —Anthony, age 27

You won't be able to fly solo in the lab, the factory, or the office. If you do, your input will be disregarded or even sabotaged. You will be viewed as arrogant and ignorant. However, the extent to which your value depends on your ability to coordinate with others will vary according to what you're doing and where. In some jobs, your effectiveness is totally dependent on teamwork.

I became assistant brand manager, a plum job. But it was 100 percent responsibility with no authority. Whatever I wanted done, I had to ease it through the other departments rather than try to impose it.

—Brent, age 28

In your college jobs and internships, you need to gain skills and confidence in collaborating with others.

If you find this difficult and unpleasant, or if you feel a strong need to be independent in your actions and results, you'll have to turn your search towards work that affords you greater isolation and control. Many service jobs and positions where you contribute a specialized technical expertise, as well as some sales jobs can permit you to make an independent contribution.

Can You Stand Being Bossed Around?

In school and college, the teacher tells you what to do and then grades you. But once you get to college, no one is bossing you around. Whether or not you go to class or do your homework, you have a great deal of freedom, and you probably appreciate that a great deal. You may work some hours after class and get told what to do, and you may have a summer job where you resent the close supervision, but you know it will end.

Here too, the regular working environment is something else. You are expected to follow direction, and depending on the industry and job, this direction may be very intense and precise.

I had some experience in designing clothes, and I thought of it as a field where I could be a little creative. I couldn't believe it. She was all over me, all the time. I felt like a robot or a slave.

—Henry, age 23

Perhaps Henry can find a boss who is willing to stand back a bit and give him some room to breathe and create. But in his industry, he's not soon going to have the opportunity to go out on his own and sell his designs. If Henry has a great need for autonomy in his work, he has gone into the wrong field.

Getting bossed around affects not just the content of the work, but the process and conditions of the work as well.

He made it clear I had to be there all the time, in case he wanted me. The place was noisy. I had no room to spread out, and I was interrupted all the time. Scarcely any chance to think. Where's the exit?

—Simon, age 24

Experience with jobs, plus some imagination on your part, can tell you quite a bit about how sensitive you are to the subordination and loss of independence that is part of the price of your paycheck. Even within very large organizations, there are some activities, especially sales and service, where you're largely on your own. Other kinds of work, such as teaching and programming, also can offer a great deal of freedom from day to day supervision. If you enter such a profession you will have considerable latitude in how you do your work, although not nearly as much as you would have had 20 or 30 years ago.

I get sent to different client locations to update their systems, and I only see my boss every couple of weeks. How I do the job is strictly up to me. I wouldn't want it any other way.

—Ned, age 27

Multitasking

As a student, you're used to juggling four or more classes, not just over the course of a term, but from day to day. Jobs vary in the extent to which they require you to divide your attention over a few or many different projects and demands. Many people have a strong preference for a work life that is tightly focused rather than diffused over numerous activities.

Just keeping this little operation running is a big sweat. Every day not just one thing but many things go wrong. A contractor is late, or an employee or a customer has a big, urgent problem. I am just "Mr. Fix-It."

—Peter, age 29

What is not apparent, even from talking to Peter, is whether he really thrives on this kind of existence or whether he feels that it's wearing him out. But you may have stronger opinions on the subject. If so, make sure you get in touch with yourself, and aim at jobs that will be compatible with your preferences.

What is it like to work "on the platform" of a bank branch? Indescribable. One constant hassle. An overdraft, a delayed deposit, and you're always being pulled out on a limb. Thank God I got a transfer to Marketing!

—Clarence, age 25

Not every marketing job is hassle free. But if you want to be able to keep your eye fixed on a goal, with a minimum of interruptions and conflicting priorities, then you may find yourself most comfortable in development work, in some staff functions such as finance, and in a large organization rather a small one. If you thrive on tackling multiple and unpredictable demands, you can have a great career in almost any aspect of operations and service.

These are just some of the major considerations you need to take into account when pondering your future. Bear in mind that you may not know what you like or hate on the job until you try it. Be a little adventurous. Try internships, volunteer work, or part-time jobs that will require you to develop new skills and try new things. You may have talents you never knew about.

What Do You Want from Your Job—And Your Life?

3

The previous chapter called attention to characteristics of jobs that you might find either appealing or unappealing, characteristics that might makes some jobs much better suited than others to your capabilities and preferences. What wasn't discussed there was the vast differences between the various rewards offered by different jobs. Such rewards can include pay, prospects for advancement, and prestige, as well as freedom from stress and constraints.

The content and requirements of a job may match your interests and preferences very well as far as the work itself is concerned, but the job may nevertheless fail to offer the pay level or the possibilities for advancement that you require in order to be satisfied. For instance, teaching in a nursery school may be engaging, entertaining, and personally rewarding, but the pay may not be enough for you to live in the way that you feel you need to live. Other jobs may offer one of the rewards you want, while not providing another of the rewards you find essential. For instance, work on a garbage truck pays very well. The job itself might not bother you, but you would probably not be happy having your friends and family know you did it.

I have an older friend who has become a diamond cutter and dealer. He likes the work and the independence, and he makes extremely good money. But I'm not willing to join him. It's just not the place for an educated person, it seems to me.

—Paul, age 22

As in committing to a college, or to a spouse, the job or career that you choose is unlikely to respond ideally to all your desires. Hence, you need to make tradeoffs, giving up one benefit in order to gain another. You may settle for a husband who is not ideally handsome or even ideally sexy, because he's extremely kind and loving. Likewise, you might choose a job that is extremely satisfying and enjoyable even though it pays less than you would like to make. But the tradeoff has its limits. If you take a fascinating and fulfilling job that pays so little that you can't even live decently, then you may very well regret that choice and have to make a change later.

> Your job and career will be so important in your life that in order to make choices about jobs, you really have to think more broadly about your overall life goals.

Some individuals are confident that they can be happy with a very modest lifestyle if their work is stimulating, satisfying, and free of undue pressure and demands. Others have very high ambitions for material success, ambitions that can be satisfied only by careers that will entail considerable risk, stress, and inflexibility. For most people, but by no means all, key long-term objectives include meaningful, productive, and progressively responsible work yielding economic rewards that will securely support a pleasant, middle-class lifestyle with a family. But a significant minority choose different goals and pursue them with courage and independence.

I've started a little magazine and I'm very committed to using it to express my point of view. I'll never make enough money to have children or a lot of possessions, but I'm absolutely certain that that's going to be okay. My fiancé agrees.

—Christine, age 26

In making these choices, it's necessary to be honest with yourself rather than assume that you're a superperson or martyr. It's also necessary go beyond honesty about the person you are today in order to think clearly and logically about the person you will become in three years or thirteen years. Everyone wants immediate gratification, and the near future is much more predictable than the more distant future. However, if you take a job that will be interesting and well enough paid today, but that offers very little hope of keeping up with your needs and facilitating your growth in responsibility and compensation as you grow older, then you're likely to regret this decision later.

Think, then, about the life you want to have—first during the few years after graduation, and then beyond. You have probably visualized or daydreamed about that life, but it's important to distinguish realistic goals from daydreams. You may be able to see yourself as a best-selling author, a world-renowned professor, or a famous financial tycoon. But, are those ambitions that you can pursue with confidence and realism, or are they pipe dreams? When you're young, there are risks that are worth taking because at worst you can back up and start again. There are other risks that would be foolish to accept because the prospects of reward are slight, and the penalties for failure are serious. Those are the distinctions you need to draw.

I love to play the violin, but I'm not good enough to become a soloist. At best, I'd be buried forever in the depths of a good orchestra. In the beginning, the pay is great, but I know that even with chamber music and teaching, I'd get frustrated at the limited outlets for individual expression, so I won't do it.

—*Clarine, age 23*

Identifying the Rewards You Need

In order to make appropriate tradeoffs and target job goals that fit your needs as well as your preferences for the work itself, you first have to survey your lifestyle needs to make sure that all the important requirements have been identified. Here are some that are important to many recent graduates, but you may have others that are equally or even more important to you.

Immediate Financial Compensation

This is likely to be one of your needs.

If I just put a few full-time years into my photography, pursing my own artistic goals, I'm confident I could start selling it well. My parents and even my girlfriend have offered to make that possible, but I'm absolutely not willing to prolong my dependence on others. Photography will be a hobby, and it won't be or affect my career.

—*Scott, age 22*

Prestige and Social Consequences

This may not be in line with its monetary rewards. It can be important to you to do work that is respected, so that you yourself can be respected.

> *What I've always wanted to do is run a small store where I sell really nice things that people like me want to buy. But everyone I know thinks it's just creepy to run a store. I'm tired of trying to explain it.*
>
> —*Judith, age 21*

Freedom from Risk, Pressure, and Constraints

These are job characteristics that many, but not all of us, strongly desire.

> *I was offered the opportunity to work in a prominent trading and arbitrage firm. It's like a 24-hour-a-day responsibility, the risks are high, and you're tied to your equipment. I don't think I could do that, even for a few years.*
>
> —*Richard, age 23*

Other people—much fewer of them—feel they thrive on stress and seek it out.

> *When I'm given a month, I coast uncomfortably for the first three weeks. I need a job where I have to produce every day, every hour. That makes the juices flow. I love it.*
>
> —*Bea, age 25*

Upward Mobility

Upward mobility means prospects for greater responsibility and compensation as your career progresses. Upward mobility means that you become more valuable with experience, and you're rewarded for this value. Most people are reluctant to sacrifice the expectation of career growth.

> *I was thinking of medicine, specifically pediatrics. But the way the system is evolving, I think I'd go out where I came in. After 15 or 25 years, will I be more valuable? If not, I think I'll be unhappy.*
>
> —*Erica, age 21*

Everyone's need for each of these rewards is different. Each differs as to how much of each he is willing to give up in order to have a job and career where the job content itself is stimulating and satisfying.

Personal Gratification

The feeling that you're doing something meaningful is very important to some people. Unfortunately, some very satisfying jobs, like teaching or social work, pay very little. To pursue such a career, your own pride in your work and your belief that you're making the world a better place must compensate for the limited material rewards you will receive.

> *My desire to help people is going to be expressed through a career in social work. I won't get rich, and certain people will hate me for what I do, even some clients. None of that matters. I've tried it, and for me the satisfactions are overwhelming, so I'm not really sacrificing anything.*
>
> —*Patrick, age 23*

What Happens If You Take A Job That Cannot Meet Your Needs?

Scientists say that a bumblebee can give attention to only one thing at a time. It just flies towards a flower. We humans are supposed to be better able to take account of several factors at once. That is what we need to do in sorting out job possibilities, rather than just aiming for the sweetest or nearest one.

A Great Job, But Not Enough Pay

It's a wonderful feeling to earn and deposit your first regular paycheck. But what happens when you find that it's not enough to meet even your minimum expenses?

> *While I was in college I took the necessary teacher-training courses because I knew I loved being with kids and I felt I had something to give. Now, after two years of teaching math in a fine private school, I love my work more and more. But I see that it's going to be very hard for me to have the simple things I need—a decent apartment, a car that runs—if I continue as a teacher. I would have to depend on my boyfriend's income. So, I've been thinking about going into accounting, but I don't know much about it.*
>
> *—Ellen, age 26*

Ellen was able to begin taking accounting courses in the evening. Somewhat to her surprise, she found accounting to be intellectually challenging but well suited to her abilities. After three semesters, she was hired by one of the largest national public accounting firms as a junior auditor. She was several years older than almost everyone else at her level in the firm, but that situation neither embarrassed nor disadvantaged her. Her greater maturity helped her stand out.

Would Ellen have been better off using her college years somewhat differently? Probably. In some ways, her position is a good one. She most likely has 35 or 40 years of work ahead of her. The fact that her accounting career started a few years "late" is not likely to stunt her professional growth or limit her opportunities. The success in teaching enhanced her confidence in her communication skills and gave her a professional position that she could later fall back on.

But Ellen should look forward as well as back. She went into her accounting job with a very limited professional and technical background. She knows almost nothing about other fields and functions of business, and that's disadvantageous for an accountant. Of course, she can go on learning. But at Cal Berkeley, she could have taken a number of excellent business courses during her last two college years, as well as pursuing part-time employment and internship opportunities. (Many other colleges, including most Ivies, have much less to offer undergraduates interested in business. Those students have to search out their business education during the summer, or off campus.)

Exploring business during her college years, Ellen might well have developed other interests within the domain of management that were equally or better aligned with her bent towards math, towards people, and even towards teaching. These might have ranged from human resources management and training to financial analysis, marketing, insurance actuarial work, and even consulting. Yes, she has made a successful start at changing careers, and rather quickly and easily at that. But has she found the "right" career, the one that will best leverage her interests in order to fulfill her goals? Or has she merely migrated rather hurriedly from an unsuitable job to one that she will find tolerable for a while? Is it going to be equally easy for her to make another change to get closer to a higher-valued target? Or will Ellen have to worry about being stigmatized as flighty if she contemplates a still further change, away from public accounting?

Talking with Ellen again to establish a wider perspective on these questions, you would learn that before graduating from college, she had not acquired much information about the practical aspects of her targeted career, teaching. For instance, although she knew something about what public school teachers were paid, she wrongly assumed that private school teachers are paid more. In reality many are paid less because their jobs are more prestigious and pleasant. Furthermore, the great majority of teachers are paid almost entirely on the basis of seniority, not merit, a fact of which Ellen was unaware.

Ellen never figured out how much money she was going to have after taxes, and how much she would need to live in the way she wanted. In fact, her rough estimate of monthly earnings didn't include income taxes.

Looking ahead, Ellen is already beginning to chafe at the rather rigid rules and hierarchy that typify large accounting firms. One of the things that appealed to her about teaching was the opportunity for independence and initiative, and the freedom from day-to-day supervision at work. Whether in the long run she can adapt to or put up with a virtually military job environment is doubtful. Of course, if she sticks it out for a few years, she could move to a smaller and more flexible firm or even start her own accounting business. But that will involve additional challenges and risks, of which she knows nothing yet.

Had Ellen interned at an accounting firm or spoken in depth with a few people in their first few years of work at such firms, she would have known what to expect. But Ellen felt she was already behind, and she was keen to make a change quickly. Indeed, so sweeping a career change may well feel wrenching and traumatic, even at the age of 25. "What will I tell my friends and the people I work with?" is the least of the problems. Ellen's situation and prospects could be worse, but they certainly could be better, especially considering her multiple talents and her attractive personality.

Plenty of Money, More Than Enough Stress: Too Much Job

Almost all of us need to earn some amount of money from our work. Nonetheless, most people, certainly including Ellen, don't enshrine money as their highest value, and they have no interest in simply picking whatever job appears to offer the most money.

> It is important to work out how much you need, and this differs from one person to another and depends among other things on living costs in different locations as well as family situation.

Ellen's first job gave her plenty of job satisfaction and independence, but not enough money. The opposite also happens: plenty of money, but a job that takes too much out of your life and gives too little back.

> *I became an executive recruiter almost by accident, but the pay was great and it kept getting better. I was a high flyer, and I went first class. They had talked up my becoming a partner, and I finally did. That's about when I figured out that I was spending all my time on planes, on call for foreign clients 24 hours a day, increasingly out of touch with my family. The work was a meaningless blur, and I wound up with a very destructive divorce.*

Now I've quit. I'm thinking about what I want to do with the rest of my life.

—Luther, age 37

Working life is lived one day at a time. What begins as exciting and rewarding can become very gradually more harried, and less meaningful. Eventually, something snaps. A marriage breaks down, a career is terminated. It's hard to pinpoint any one big mistake that Luther made, but he's not a happy man, and one can't really say he was just unlucky.

If Luther had been more explicit about his needs and values, not just at the beginning of his career but thereafter, then he might have been able to regain control of his life and turn it in a more positive direction. Because Luther failed to manage his career, even at the beginning, the career increasingly dominated the man. At no time did he find enough time to give real attention and initiative to possibilities such as moderating his work load or taking a job where the skills he had developed could be exercised in a less pressured environment. The career that he began "almost by accident" ended with a crash.

The Job Fits Fine, But It Won't Grow

Sometimes it's possible to find a job that fits as snugly and comfortably as a snail's shell. It accommodates your interests and capabilities, it gives you the pay and position you need. But, if the shell can't grow, it will eventually have to be discarded. That can leave you without a place to work, and vulnerable.

I grew up on a farm and I love farming. But I could see that the risk and the stress were too much for me. So, I decided to become a county agricultural agent, a civil servant whose job is to help farmers get the resources and knowledge needed for success. I find the work very satisfying, and the pay was enough for me to get married and start a family. But I now see that my prospects for promotion are very limited. And unless I improve my income, my family will be sacrificing too much. This is very painful.

—Richard, age 29

Richard had targeted an initial career path about which he was quite well informed. His short-term goal was attainable, and he correctly anticipated that he would like the work. From the standpoint of lifestyle, the choice not only seemed ideal but actually was ideal for him—in the short run. But there always is a tomorrow, and in fact a great many of them.

> In your job interviews, you're likely to be asked: "What do you see yourself doing in five or ten years?" This is a test of whether you have thought ahead at all, or with any realism.

You need a good answer, and this answer is likely to vary from one interview to another. Richard could and perhaps did give a fine answer to that question. But satisfying an interviewer in a couple of minutes of give-and-take is one thing, and satisfying yourself over a period of years is something else.

How could Richard have avoided what became, for him, a dead-end job? Once he got seriously interested in this specific job, he could have called up and informally interviewed several people who were already doing the job. Without being at all confrontational, Richard could have raised the key questions about his future prospects. The agents with whom he spoke could have provided both factual information and a more subjective perspective. In fact, Richard was already well acquainted with a few agents—too well acquainted, in fact, to feel comfortable in asking the crucial questions about compensation and promotion prospects. So he didn't ask.

Even before this, Richard could probably have gotten data, both orally and in writing, from the relevant Civil Service and personnel offices. This information typically shows how many positions there are at each level; salary ranges; and the promotion routes and requirements. This would have been helpful preparation for Richard's conversations with current holders of his tentatively targeted job.

Information about the age of job holders, even if incomplete or informal, can be especially helpful in identifying jobs that afford very limited opportunity for progression. If Richard found that within a few years, he would be at a level largely populated by people over 40, this might have given him a broad hint that he would find it difficult to move any further up.

Richard's experience shows that it's possible to home in prematurely on a choice of job that is one-dimensional. You may understand your dream job very well, but you need to look both beyond it and on both sides of the road. If you want to make a change, where will you be employable? Will you be progressively enhancing your skills and market value? Aiming at exactly one job is almost never the right answer. It will likely be as bad as aiming for no job at all.

There's Such a Thing as Being Too Picky

The last few interviews above demonstrate the value of thought and caution in riveting yourself to a job. Seen in that light, these stories can help you . . . but they don't imply that you should avoid focusing your preparations for work until you're confident you have found a job that will surely meet all your needs. If you demand too much from your first job, the analysis may paralyze rather than empower you. Think, but don't fail to decide and to act.

If you can't find a job track that satisfies all of your needs, you may be failing to focus positively on the numerous possibilities open to you. Taking an expedient short-term job can be a prelude to years of unstable and marginal employment. One 28-year-old woman, Carole, an honors graduate in political science, had a résumé that included five different employers in seven years. (And even with this many employers, there were gaps.) Looking at the nature of her employers and of her tasks, it seems as if Carole had been careful to avoid anything that could readily have become a permanent or career job.

Carole had recently gone back to get an M.A. in French studies, but this had been followed by two more marginal jobs. There was no long-term employment, much less a career, anywhere in sight. She wasn't advancing towards greater responsibility and accomplishment.

> *To me, a job is just a job. It's a way of using your skills and earning a living. A career is a series of jobs. I find opportunities, but no one of them really turns out to fit. I don't gain any traction or momentum, and the job ends. I'm confused.*

—*Carole, age 28*

Although her words sound cynical, Carole is something of an idealist: She started each of her jobs with unrealistic hopes, though in fact each time she had backed into the job rather than seeking it out. This may continue until Carole observes that an unconnected succession of jobs doesn't constitute a career. There needs to be an underlying theme and direction that gives purpose to the endeavor. Carole has never committed, even provisionally, to answering the key questions of who she is and what she wants out of her life and work. To progress, you don't need a particular dollar amount or title or accomplishment as an ultimate goal, but you need a sense of what you want and where to find it.

Another interviewee, Bruce, had been much more positive than Carole about his career ideas. But not one of them lasted. He had aimed at medicine, until he took organic chemistry (in which, oddly enough, he got an A). Then he was attracted to physical anthropology, later to forensic science, and finally to geology. Meanwhile, Bruce became an "over-30."

For nine years, he had earned a basic living and done some volunteer work in one or another of the fields he studied. But with all this, at least in hindsight, there had never been a "first job" that offered a route, a trajectory into a lasting career. More than 20 percent of the graduates who completed interviews had failed to move directly from college into a career-building first job. Why?

It's easy to blame such people for an unwillingness to commit, or for stalling, or for a lack of interest in working hard for a prolonged period. Another view would be that both Carole and Bruce did what was comfortable for them from day to day, and did it without regrets. But in both cases, a lot of talent and energy remained untapped. Both of these people are achievers. They could easily have accomplished much more and thereby gained much greater satisfaction.

What was lacking in each case was realistic, fact-based decision making, with consistency in setting job goals and moving towards these goals. Lack of discipline in decision making inevitably leads either to casual, whimsical choices, or to decisions made under time pressure. These decisions can at best meet immediate needs, with no more than a scant and vague hope of opening a route towards a career that will satisfy long-term objectives.

But Bruce didn't have to worry, because he never had trouble getting work.

> *When I have an interest, I figure out where there is a job. I never have trouble getting a job, because I care about what I do. One time I walked right in to the county coroner and got him to hire me to do dissections. I was excited, but it turned out I didn't like the job. I'm used to that, but it's getting discouraging.*

> —*Bruce, age 32*

That's another special thing about Bruce and Carole: Both of them are not bad at getting hired. Far from it. They're always full of enthusiasm, and they know what they're talking about. It's almost too easy for them to move on and find another job that, for the moment, seems appealing. In a way, they're victims of their own plausibility, fluency, and flexibility.

For a person who is going to graduate from college, almost any sensible and considered decision, implemented soundly and realistically in the context of long term objectives, is likely to work out better than taking a job just because it's there and is momentarily appealing.

Working Out Your Objectives

Your decisions about how to direct your energy and spend your time in college need to reflect your job goals, and these in turn must be consistent with your objectives, the rewards you seek from your life and your career. Realism in setting objectives begins with observation of those around you, and self questioning as to how your wants and needs would or would not be satisfied by the rewards and constraints these other people face. Normally, the people about whom you know the most are your parents.

Would you be satisfied with their material lifestyle? Do you want to work as hard as they do? Do they find their work interesting and fulfilling? Would you? You can and should ask these questions about anyone who is within your range of close observation, but you will very likely know more about your parents than about others.

Most of us have no appetite for the jobs that we feel we know the most about.

> *My father was a lawyer. From my earliest years, I knew that his work was uninteresting, I never heard anything fun about it. Knowing I wouldn't like law put me a step ahead. I have no regrets. I like my work, and it isn't law.*

—*Bob, age 58*

That's par for the course. But your natural desire to establish an identity distinct from your parents shouldn't cloud your judgment about jobs. Maybe Bob's father was bored by the law and gave Bob an overly negative impression of the trade. The grass is often greener on the other side of the fence. You have to try to make allowances for that, and, in particular, to get closer to the jobs that appeal to you in order to see whether their appeal dissolves when you learn more.

Some students find their parents' work downright embarrassing.

> *My father is . . . well, basically, he's a life insurance agent, though they have a fancier name for it now. I wince when I hear him tell people what he does. The part I really couldn't do is calling people up, chasing them, pushing them to buy more insurance.*

—*Sandy, age 22*

Sandy is obviously worried about prestige, as well as about whether she can do or would like the work. This worry may invite Sandy to think harder about what other kinds of jobs would embarrass her, and about how important it is for her to have a job she's proud of.

It's helpful to talk to as many other people as are accessible to you—relatives, family friends, people with whose businesses you are in contact—to learn more about what they do and what they get out of it. Visit them at work, ask questions, and spend a morning or a day seeing what happens. You don't have to ask, "What do you earn?" You can ask, "What would I earn?"

Another place very definitely worth visiting is the career counseling office on your campus. They are there to help you, they are professionals in this field, and they are probably freer from bias for or against any particular career than is anyone else you can find. They can administer tests that assess the fit of your interests and desires with various occupations, and they can give you more subjective feedback through discussion and by responding to your questions. They also have a great deal of information about jobs and careers, both statistical and descriptive.

Do not ever be reluctant or embarrassed to ask for this help. Few people are absolutely certain what to do with their lives. Unbiased feedback on your ideas is a virtual necessity for sound decision making. If you don't agree with the advice you get, you won't have to follow it.

Does It Matter Where You Went to College?

4

If you're interested in a career in technology, your career starts in high school. The most important thing about your background when you apply for your first job out of college will be where you went to college. If you went to a second-tier school, you'll have a much more difficult time presenting yourself to recruiters.

—Alan Manuel, *cofounder of Cductive.com, age 30*

"Your career starts in high school"? That sounds awfully discouraging. What does Alan mean by that? Is it too late if you are already in college but don't feel your career has started yet?

First of all, in today's superheated competitive environment, if you want to be a hot shot and, for instance, co-found a successful technology company (as Alan did) by the time you're 30, then you had better move fast. You should have good AP scores in subjects such as Calculus BC and Physics C before you enter college. But beyond that, you have an advantage if you have gotten into one of the first-tier colleges. And doing that, of course, depends on what and how you did while you were still in high school.

If you are graduating from a college thought to be less excellent, then recruiters may tend to play the averages and discriminate against you, no matter how bright, achieving, and well trained you might be. Many of the "best" jobs will go to the people who went to the colleges that these recruiters consider the "best" colleges, whether or not the colleges deserve this preferential treatment.

> We will do most of our hiring at the same colleges this year as last year, and it's been that way for quite a while. We're comfortable with the quality of the students, and we know how to read the transcripts. If our needs increase, we'll look more widely.
>
> —Corporate recruiter, age 31

Your choice of college can certainly affect the job offers you get, directly as well as indirectly. You were at least vaguely aware of that fact when you decided where to apply. Most likely your first-choice college was more selective and relatively hard for you to get into. It was the type of college that would be more likely to impress people—including you, and including potential employers. Your last-choice college, the one you were almost sure to get into, would be seen by almost everyone as a less impressive one.

Some employers are glad to let selective colleges take the responsibility for picking the best students, because the employers assume that these best students will become the best job candidates. After all, it's easier for a manager to explain to his boss why he made an offer to someone from a college that is in great demand than to explain why he made that same offer to a person who went to a college that is less respected.

The college you enter can thus make it easier or harder for you to get some jobs, but not all. There are employers who prefer smaller or local colleges, or who have special relationships with colleges that are not necessarily the ones most sought after by students.

> *Frankly, our CEO went to Louisiana State University. A fine school, you know? We look especially closely to hire plenty of kids from LSU, and particularly from the big teams there, such as basketball. We feel more comfortable with LSU than with Harvard. I have no problem with that.*

> —*Corporate human resources manager, age 44*

Some recruiters—as well as some CEOs—love "good old State" or another local school. They may also find it more comfortable and expedient to make offers to students at a college where their recruiters have a personal knowledge of classes, grading patterns, student organizations, and even professors. When several students are hired from the same campus every year, there can be a continuity of friendships and information.

> *When I'm interviewing, I want to bring the student onto common ground, where I know what he's talking about and I can apply some reality checks. It's hard to do that at a campus where I don't even know my way to the interview room. It's easiest to do it at my own school—and I like the feeling that I'm helping students there.*

> —*Barbara, age 25*

There are also employers, such as big car rental companies, who need to recruit on a very large scale and are happy to consider graduates of any accredited college, most likely on an evenhanded basis. These jobs don't tend to be the most glamorous ones, but they can give you a way to get into the thick of things and show what you can do. There are obvious advantages to working with employers who are reaching to find enough people to fill their needs, as opposed to employers who are inundated with applicants and would just as soon make most of them disappear.

> *Frankly, we* pay *people to get us applications and résumés from qualified students. We're not picky about colleges. If we're leaving anyone out, tell me about it!*

—*Manager, college relations, major corporation*

Around one third of recent graduates interviewed for this book felt that their choice of college had limited their job possibilities.

Whether or not you end up pleased with your job search results, you probably won't blame your college for making you look less than first rate. However, your college can also affect your job possibilities in less obvious ways.

Your Campus Placement Office: A Forgotten Resource

When you were deciding where to apply to college, you undoubtedly gave some weight to your ideas about the academic quality of the schools you were considering. You may also have considered sports, activities, and other aspects of what a college offers. But there's another crucial facility that you probably didn't think about at all. It's known as the college placement office, or something similar on your campus. Perhaps you have not even noticed that such a place exists at your school. If so, you'd better rectify your oversight—pronto.

> *The first time I went to the placement office was in the fall of my senior year, when I was told to go there by a prospective employer. I can see now I had things turned around. It should have been the placement office telling me about employers!*
>
> —*Patsy, age 23*

The placement office provides the means by which a college helps its students gain desirable employment when they graduate. It welcomes recruiters for corporations and other employers, assists in the flow of information and the interviewing process, and helps students learn about employment possibilities. Perhaps this makes it sound as if a placement office is merely a frill or an option. That is not the case, though there still seem to be some colleges that imagine this to be true.

> Your placement office is very likely to play a crucial role in finding the job you want.

As a practical matter, most placement offices are able to do this only if you get a job during the months preceding your graduation. Very few colleges offer much practical assistance to alumni in finding a first or subsequent job at a later time. Some placement offices or other college bureaus do offer limited help in finding summer employment or term-time work.

> *If I had it to do over again, honestly, I'd have "interviewed" the placement offices before deciding where to go to college. Some of my*

friends at nearby colleges are getting all kinds of help that I'm just not getting. And they're getting much better access to interviews. Everything here is late and overcrowded.

—*Harriet, age 21*

Getting your first job is not the primary purpose of your college experience (at least, not from the faculty's standpoint). But college has no legitimate purpose that should conflict with or obstruct your efforts to achieve the best possible access to jobs. Work out what you need in the way of help, and go after it.

The sooner you get to know the capabilities of your placement office and those of the people in it, the better. During the job hunting season, when the office is busiest, you will need these people to give you one kind of help or another; for instance, to find a place for you on a list of interviewees that's already full. Or to send your résumé to a company even though you don't satisfy all their requirements. So, make yourself favorably known as far in advance as possible, show interest, be cooperative, and help out if possible. Most companies have no interest in what the placement folks think of one applicant versus another, but the placement office can find other places to put their thumb on the scale.

I went to the placement office when I was a freshman to find out about summer internships. I made a point of hanging around and meeting the staff. I even helped with the filing from time to time. As a result, I was actually able to help get some interesting companies to begin recruiting here, and in a couple of cases they were able to put my name near the top of the list in a subliminal way.

—*Peggy, age 21*

The placement office usually doesn't rank high in popularity and importance in the eyes of the faculty or the administration of a college. It costs money and doesn't appear to be a part of a liberal education. It's precisely because the placement office is a low-prestige, underfunded operation that your involvement there will be appreciated and rewarded. Of the interviewees who were very pleased with their first job, more than 25 percent attributed this happy outcome at least partially to an unusually intense involvement with their placement office.

> *I made a point of talking to the people in the placement office who are in direct contact with corporate recruiters. Many of these recruiters have something to say about what they are looking for that isn't fully expressed in the printed literature. If you know something about their concerns and hot buttons, you can tune your interviewing style and even your résumé accordingly.*

—*Tom, age 23*

The Role of the Placement Office

Companies that wish to recruit graduating seniors are encouraged to contact the placement office. The placement office lists the positions offered by these companies, generally in return for a fee charged to the companies. Company recruitment materials are then made available through the placement office. A student who believes she qualifies for a position arranges for her résumé, and perhaps other materials such as a transcript and recommendations, to be compiled by the placement office. The placement office provides this material to the employer together with similar material for the other students who are interested in the same position. Thus, the employer receives a set of files containing relatively uniform material on each candidate from your school who is competing for the position.

The employer then decides which of your school's candidates will be offered initial interviews. If these interviews are to be held on campus, the placement office generally arranges for the interview rooms and asks the invited applicants to sign up for interview times. On-campus facilities and times are generally quite limited, and these limitations may determine the number of students who can be interviewed. Of course, it's also possible for companies to rent space in a nearby hotel, but this is less convenient for students and harder to coordinate.

Where possible, employers generally choose fairly recent graduates of your college or other nearby colleges to do the initial on-campus interviewing. After the first round of interviews (and possibly a second round of on-campus interviews for those students who survived the cut after the first round), the role of the placement office diminishes. Contacts are usually pursued directly between the companies and the students, leading to hiring decisions.

> *After the first or second round, the company has invested some effort in you, and they're beginning to think about how to get you motivated to accept an offer if they make one. So, they call or leave messages for you directly.*

> —*Renee, age 22*

The decision to begin the recruiting process by interviewing on campus represents a substantial commitment of resources on the part of the employer. This is often backed up by further efforts aimed at attracting a strong group of applicants. The company may advertise in the school newspaper to persuade interested students to sign up with the placement office. It may also run an evening information session to meet and encourage potential applicants.

At a minimum, the company will be sending employees to spend days of their time conducting interviews. Obviously this makes sense only if the company intends to hire. While the exact number of students to be hired from each campus is not generally determined in advance, the purpose of the interviewing is to recruit. If an employer interviews on any campuses at all, and most major employers do, then they generally interview on all campuses where they expect to hire a significant number of students. Hence, a considerable fraction of the total hiring of current graduates is accomplished through the on-campus process.

We fill up to 80 percent of our posts for new grads through on-campus recruiting. It gives us better comparability between candidates, and it's much more efficient than having people show up at all different times and places.

—Corporate recruiter, technology industry

In the most recent Job Outlook survey conducted by the National Association of Colleges and Employers (NACE) of companies seeking to hire college graduates, on-campus recruiting was rated the most important recruiting technique—far more important than either advertising or the solicitation of applications by current employees.

To a great extent your immediate employment opportunities, or at least your opportunities to work for large companies with specialized requirements, *are determined by the list of employers who interview on your campus.* One reason for this is your own limited time and need for efficiency and convenience. If plenty of interviews are available on campus, and if you feel hard pressed to keep up these opportunities while doing justice to your classes and activities, then you won't be eager to search out even more interviews.

> *I had plenty to do researching the companies I signed up to interview with on campus. I really can't imagine studying all the other companies and going around to see them. I don't know anyone who did that.*

—*Brett, age 21*

It's less convenient to chase after companies that don't come to your campus. It's also less likely that you can get offers this way.

Here's an example: Suppose you are a student at Penn State, and a company you are interested in recruits on campus at the University of Pennsylvania, but not at Penn State. This may not be because they like Penn better. It may be because of convenience factors, student population, and the number of applicants the company wants. Or, it may simply reflect old habits or any number of other factors, including limited capacity at your placement office. Whatever the reason for the employer's decision, the result is that it will be substantially harder for you to be hired as a Penn State student than it would have been had you become a University of Pennsylvania student.

Here's why: As a Penn State student, you won't be able to interview on campus. So, unless you have some personal connection with the company, you will have to write in and send your résumé. Such a résumé is not likely to receive the same consideration that it would if it came from a placement office. One reason for this is that the résumés that come from placement offices have been solicited. The employer is committed to choosing from among them the group who will be interviewed on campus. Generally this selection is done in a fairly systematic way, with attention to GPA and perhaps to major, as well as to work experience. If you are among the top 20 or top 100 candidates from your campus, then you can count on getting over this first and highest hurdle and receiving an interview.

> *When you go through the placement office, the employers just want a standard package . . . it's no work. Outside the placement office, you need a cover letter and can expect to do plenty of calling. How much of that is it worth doing?*
>
> *—Sol, age 22*

Something other than laziness is involved. If you have to mail in your résumé, the first person to see it is probably not looking for students to interview, but rather for a reason to toss away one more piece of mail and get through the stack more quickly. After all, most or all of the positions available can be filled by the on-campus process, so there's no need to look hard to find interesting candidates in the daily mail. Furthermore, an off-campus interview, even if you beat the odds and are granted one, is likely to be less convenient and more time consuming for you to attend.

The flip side to the Penn State problem is that if you are a student there, your placement office will have plenty of employers interviewing. Although these may not be precisely the companies that you would have chosen for yourself, it's a heck of a lot easier to make your choices from this menu than it is to slog through a directory of corporations. That becomes very clear after you hear enough discouraging stories from classmates or older people who have mailed out 100 résumés and gotten zero interviews. So, you need to recognize that there's a high probability that your ultimate employer will be one of the companies that comes to your campus.

In a recent survey conducted by the University of Illinois Alumni Career Center asking employers to rank 12 methods for recruitment of college candidates, on-campus recruiting was ranked Number 1. Career days and job fairs were ranked Number 2. "Unsolicited applications" was ranked nearly at the bottom.

Go Where the Employers Are

You can already anticipate the punchline here. The most important single thing about your placement office is not the nice, knowledgeable, helpful staff. Neither is it their fine library of company brochures and "how to get a job" books. No, the most important thing about your placement office is the number and the quality of the companies that it hosts at your campus, and the number of interviews they conduct. The list changes somewhat from year to year—hopefully, it expands. But last year's list will give you a good enough idea of what is to come. Indeed, the list of employers who are interested enough in students like you to visit your campus might just constitute the single most important benefit of your placement office. It could even turn out to be the most important thing about your college—at least as regards the college's impact on your initial job-hunting success.

I asked about some companies that weren't on the list. The answer was that "we have a limited number of slots." Companies that interviewed last year get first crack. It seems to me slots should be based on how many they hired.

—Wendy, age 22

If you want to do something tomorrow morning that will help you get a good job, the most useful thing you can do is to go down to your placement office and get, or compile, a list of the companies that interview there. It's also worth getting the names of any companies that have asked to be included in the interview program but that could not be accommodated. These companies might be interested in hearing from you directly. But if a company has not expressed interest in interviewing, then the prospects of attracting their attention are poor.

If your placement office doesn't have a list of all the companies that visit the campus, then do some detective work, find the interview sign-up sheets. Or call some companies you are interested in and ask where they have been interviewing. If the person who answers the phone can't or won't give you the information, then someone else will. Companies with offices around the country, such as Merrill Lynch and IBM, may organize some of their recruiting through regional or even local offices.

Once you have the facts about your college's placement office and the recruitment activities it sponsors, you may be either thrilled or disappointed. At worst, you will feel that you are in the wrong place. But even if you are, you won't have to stay there.

> *I transferred from the University of Illinois after my freshman year. Although the University of Illinois is a very good technical school, I realized that I would have exposure to many more companies recruiting on campus at UVA. UVA adds credibility to my background; it's smaller and more selective and opens more doors.*
>
> *—Billy May, age 27*

Billy's experience underscores the fact that on-campus interview opportunities are not necessarily proportional to a university's size. A smaller school may snag more companies than a large one because of its reputation, its geography, or the effective management of its placement office. Indeed, of the recent graduates interviewed for this book, 55 percent of those from large universities were satisfied with their placement offices, while 68 percent of those from smaller universities and colleges felt this way.

Relationships between schools and employers are rooted in habit, if not in tradition. If a company has been hiring from the University of Virginia, then the young managers selected to do its recruiting will likely go back and recruit there rather than at some other campus they don't know as well. This is history, not logic. Do not rely on reputation, buzz, and claims. Get the facts.

A student who is job conscious may learn some important things during his freshman year and act on them. It would really have been better to learn these things still earlier, before choosing a college. But even if you are a junior or senior, your knowledge of recruiting patterns can focus your job search. Start learning about and making contact early with the companies that are most likely to offer you an interview. Reach out early to get in personal touch with managers and recruiters at any companies that are particularly interesting to you and that are unlikely to visit your school.

> *I didn't know anything about where I wanted to work because I didn't know anything about work and employers. Some people I know are going to graduate that way—ignorant. I think of them as "left footers." They're likely to start off on the wrong foot.*

—*Randy, age 21*

The great majority of students give little or no conscious thought to employment in choosing their college. That's too bad, because a little attention early in the process could help them avoid heavy effort and serious disappointment later on. Sending out large numbers of résumés and making hundreds of phone calls is not a recipe for a stimulating senior year, and the job that eludes you when you graduate may not ever come back within your sights.

How Your College Affects Your Chance of Being Interviewed

General Electric interviews at many campuses. If you want to be hired by this company, you'll want to at least visit a college where they interview. But General Electric is not likely to see all such colleges as equal—any more than you would. What this means in practice is that if General Electric interviews at any two colleges, then the unannounced standards that determine how you qualify for an interview and ultimately how you can be hired will differ between the two colleges. The differences will depend in part on the number of interview slots available and the number and quality of applicants, but they will also depend on the employer's assessment of the colleges. Corporate recruiters make no bones about the fact that your college affects your desirability.

> *The three most important things about a candidate are the school attended, the GPA, and previous work experience.*
>
> *—Eric Hutcherson, Manager of College and Diversity Relations, Lotus Development Corporation*

Of these three factors, "school attended" comes first on this particular list. That is not really a surprise. You can surely think of colleges where even if you had a 4.0 GPA, you would be a less logical hire than would a student with a 3.0 from a more selective university. It follows that even if differences in reputation and selectivity between your college and others are relatively subtle or subjective, these differences, as they are perceived by recruiters, will influence who gets the job offers.

A college president was once asked why colleges seemed to limit the number of students they take from the best high schools, while welcoming candidates from small and distant high schools that are not known for their quality. Her answer was striking: "That is what colleges mean by 'diversity.' They want students from as many high schools as possible."

Most employers don't think this way. Many want "diversity," but they have something much more concrete in mind when they use the word: affirmative action. They find it most convenient and reliable to concentrate their recruiting on a limited number of campuses, so that they are comparing apples with apples and can deploy their recruiters efficiently. If you are not in their target zone, then you are out of their sight.

A recent set of recommendations by Connie Pate, National Director of Experienced Recruiting for Ernst & Young, to employers for setting up recruiting plans suggested that the key questions under the heading of "School Selection" should be: "How well do you do at this school? How many hires are you getting?" (*Journal of Career Planning and Employment,* Spring 1998, page 35.) This is a conservative approach, and companies are generally conservative. They will do more of what was most profitable last year rather than strike out in new directions.

Results from the most recent Employer Benchmark Survey conducted by the National Association of Colleges and Employers showed that employers visited an average of 28 campuses for interviews and an average of 23 campus job fairs. Many of these are on the same campuses at which they interview.

These numbers show that you don't have to go to the highest-rated college to have access to on-campus recruiting. On the other hand, 28 is a very small fraction of the number of colleges and universities in America. From the standpoint of job-hunting opportunities, colleges are very far from equal.

It's nonetheless the case that in the past many great and important men and women, ranging from presidents to CEOs to Nobel prize winners, went to quite ordinary colleges, even small and obscure colleges, where recruitment activity was most likely minimal. The situation has not changed. Where you graduate doesn't limit where you can end up. But it can have considerable influence over where you start. If you start in the wrong place, you will be much farther from your goal. So, if you find that your choice of college will hamper your moving into the kind of job you want, then you should try to remedy that situation now instead of imagining that you can beat the odds at some later time in your career.

Your judgment needs to be based on employment patterns in the fields that are of greatest interest to you. In some fields, your college plays a lesser role in determining your employment opportunities because on-campus recruiting is less important and employers place primary reliance on other criteria in choosing among candidates.

> When I chose Cornell, I thought that where I went to college would have a huge impact on the type of job I got upon graduation. In fact, in the communications field, employers don't really care where you went to school. Relevant job experience is five times as important as where you went to school or how you did there.

—Greg Heilmann, age 24

But if the field that currently interests you most strongly is one where your college can limit your opportunities, then be realistic. This may mean a transfer, even if you are happy where you are in other respects. To transfer is drastic, and making it happen is work. But it's likely to be considerably less trouble than changing jobs later. After all, you will have less stuff to move now than later! So, if you are not satisfied with the outlook, then you need to find a way to change it. Do not think of yourself as the needle that some intrepid recruiter is going to pluck out of a haystack. Recruiters are not so magnetic.

In general, recruiters grade colleges the way students and professors do, with attention to the strength of particular departments or majors. As one example of such grading, *U.S. News and World Report* publishes an annual pecking order of colleges. But you lose more than you gain by going to a highly rated college where few of the companies you are interested in recruit.

For more specialized and technical positions, employers will rank colleges (and their graduates) according to their standing in the particular specialty for which they are recruiting. Thus, for instance, U.C. Berkeley outranks Cal Tech on most lists of colleges. However, even though U.C. Berkeley is strong in many branches of science and engineering, there are technical fields in which Cal Tech is much stronger than Berkeley. Given equal grades and experience, a company looking for a student trained in one of these fields might well be more eager to hire the Cal Tech graduate than the one from Berkeley. Most people prefer to look for a needle in a pile of needles rather than in a haystack. You may feel that as a needle, you will stand out better in the haystack than in a pile of needles, but life is not like that.

> *I got really good training in computer science, but we're not a big producer of computer scientists. The only offers I got were from the firms where I had interned and worked.*

—*Peter, age 23*

To take a more extreme case, Harvard often ranks number 1 as the nation's most selective college. But apart from an abortive effort to merge with MIT more than half a century ago—an effort that was turned down by a judge— Harvard has never given much attention to most fields of engineering, such as electrical and mechanical engineering. If you go to Harvard for "the best education" but you wind up wanting to go straight from college to an engineering job, then you are likely to find it considerably harder to get interviewed or hired than would have been the case had you gone, for example, to MIT, or even to a considerably less selective but more engineering-oriented institution. The unspoken question is, "If you're really interested in engineering, then why did you go to Harvard and stay at Harvard?" Of course, very few undergraduates at Harvard go into engineering, so this problem is not common.

> In total, there are a great many entry-level jobs for which a bachelor's degree doesn't qualify you unless you have had a special program of studies outside the liberal arts.

Although it's somewhat unfair, readers of résumés are always in a hurry. The first thing they see is the name of your college. They may jump to conclusions merely because they are unaware that MIT trains ten times as many electrical engineers as Harvard does—whether or not it trains them ten times as well. And if you want to work in electrical engineering for General Electric, you may not benefit from the fact that this corporation recruits at Harvard for "liberal arts graduates."

Thus, the case for considering making transfer applications will be a great deal stronger if, during your undergraduate years, you decide that when you graduate you want to go into a field of work for which your current college trains only a small number of people. Colleges often are particularly sympathetic to students who want to transfer for this reason, particularly if such a student makes contact with faculty in the department they want to enter and enlist their support in the application process. Furthermore, you have nothing to lose. There is ordinarily no meaningful way in which your current college can punish you for trying to transfer out. Go for it.

I hated the idea of having to go through applications all over again, and losing all my friends. But that's a heck of a lot of better than risking ending up with a lousy job where I'm not on the cutting edge. I'm glad I did it.

—*Eric, age 22*

Other Contact Points

The placement office is not necessarily the sole point of contact between employers and a college. Look for the others. Some companies sponsor scholarships, lectureships, clubs, or events. Others participate in job fairs or other campus events. Students can often play a key role in initiating a contact that later facilitates recruiting.

When I was a sophomore, I suggested that we get a speaker from Bell Labs, an organization I admire, for our engineering society. I was asked to arrange it, and I did arrange it. I worked hard to get a good turnout and a full schedule of activities. As a result, I was invited back there and offered a summer internship and later a job.

—*Ben, age 34*

A straightforward, constructive involvement with recruiting can put you on the inside track. It is not an awfully difficult task to get 50 students to say they are interested in working for a particular company. You also don't need a lot of official standing to ask companies about their interest in recruiting at your campus and to encourage them to do so. All you need to do is to start this process early enough to do yourself some good.

Remember, every company is looking for enthusiasm, and it is looking for recruiting success. You can show the necessary enthusiasm by making a contribution to the recruiting success. If the company is not working through your placement office, you might even offer to serve as an on-campus rep, signing up interested students and putting them in direct contact with the company.

What Do Your GPA and Major Have to Do with Anything?

5

We have already mentioned the fact that your résumé is more likely to be glanced at than read. When it's glanced at, just two or three facts about your college experience are likely to stand out and to be retained. One of these is the name of your college. Another is your major. And a third is your GPA, or grade point average. The GPA is a single number that sums up the quality of your academic performance.

This is a fact worth focusing on. All your reading, your homework assignments, your papers, your labs, your exams—a tremendous amount of energy and effort—gets boiled down to just a single number. That number is a summary judgment on your intelligence, your diligence and your effectiveness. For some hiring managers, GPA can even take on a kind of moral significance, as an index of your character.

However, if you feel like you have already blown your GPA beyond salvation, don't pitch yourself off a cliff just yet. A good GPA is important, but it isn't everything, as chapter 10 will show you. And there are ways to repair even a badly broken average—even if you are nearing graduation. Read on.

The most important thing I learned in college was how to discipline myself. I was able to foresee the value of grades as the point of entry for things that come later. I know of many really bright young people who simply didn't understand early enough that grades are the first screen. If they have below a certain GPA, they won't have the opportunity to compete for many opportunities for which they are otherwise qualified.

—Dr. Martin Brotman, CEO & president, California Pacific Medical Center

Taken simply as a number, your GPA may be misleading, it may be simplistic, it may be biased. But it's there. It can't be hidden or explained away. You better manage that number.

Over 80 percent of recent graduates interviewed for this book acknowledged that with a better GPA, they probably would have had a better choice of jobs.

GPA is one of the first things my firm looks at because it's an objective and quantitative measure of a candidate's ability.

—John, age 24

John works for an employer for whom success can lead to extraordinarily high compensation. Most of the people firms such as John's are going to hire will be coming into contact with the firm's clients almost immediately. They will give a favorable or unfavorable impression of the firm as a whole. Yet, such a company is not going to get to the question of how you dress or how you talk, or even of whether you know anything that will make you useful to them, until you carry them over the first hurdle. And that first hurdle is your GPA. These prestige companies will insist on seeing your GPA as a measure of your ability, whether you think it's an accurate one or not. If your GPA is not high enough for them, there will no alternative way to satisfy them, and no appeal from their decision. You probably won't even be told why you were not put on the interview list.

How Your GPA Is Computed

An intriguing fact about your GPA is that, for a while at least, you may have to compute it yourself. At Yale, for instance, official GPAs are calculated only at graduation, for use in determining honors. They are not reported on the transcripts used when you apply for jobs or internships. The placement office generally won't know your GPA through any official channel. But since employers want to have a GPA stated on your résumé, calculating it could be up to you. Check out what your own school does, and you may be surprised. Make sure you know what, if anything, will be on your transcript, and how it's computed. This could well affect some of your decisions about your studies.

> We want to see a GPA on the CV. Later on, we at least glance at the transcripts and we would notice any big discrepancy. But we don't want to wade through transcripts in making the cut for the first interview.
>
> —Corporate human resources manager

There is no uniform, official way to determine a GPA. However, there are some generally agreed upon factors in the calculation. For instance, an A is counted as 4 and a B as 3. A full-year course is counted as heavily as two semester courses or three trimester courses.

But, other aspects of the calculation are less certain. You could count an A– as a 3.67 and a B+ as 3.33, or you could count the A– as a 4 and the B+ as a 3. Courses taken on a pass/fail basis or courses not completed could be excluded entirely from the GPA calculation, or they could be counted against you. You may want to consider when to take required courses, so that they will have the most favorable effect on your GPA.

> *People often tell you to take required distribution or general education courses as soon as possible. I think that's dumb. Those big courses are hard to do well in. I saved the worst of them until I was a junior competing against freshmen, and then I had the best information and notes.*
>
> —*Peter, age 24*

If your overall GPA is impressive—well above 3.5—you have little to worry about. If some foul-ups in past courses are dragging you down, you have a couple of options. You could calculate your GPA for the most recent year, rather than for your entire college career. You could calculate the GPA for courses taken in your major, or in your major and whatever fields you consider as related ones. It would be wise to caption such figures as "Senior Year GPA," "GPA in major and related courses," and so forth. This ensures honesty. Provided you are honest, most employers are going to focus on the number, not on the adjectives and any explanations you give. People like simple statistics, and many people like to make easy comparisons and decisions based on numbers.

In fact, many employers will be particularly interested in your most recent grades because they give the most up-to-date reading on your performance. And they will be most interested in your GPA in the courses you took in your major field. After all, your work for them is going to be at least moderately specialized. It's not likely to include some poetry, some political science, and some nuclear physics. So, it's not essential that you be equally successful at everything. It's fair to expect you, by the end of college, to have figured out something that you are good at, and to have gravitated to it. Your GPA in your major shows whether you have accomplished this.

> *Today's technical methods will be outmoded in five years. However, we certainly want to see proof of the ability to learn and apply current concepts in our field. Curiosity and wide interests are a great plus, but it's nice to see that you're going into the field that you're best at.*
>
> *—Employment interviewer, large engineering company*

So, how should you handle these choices? You might want to do the calculation in the way that generates the highest GPA, provided that the result is reasonable and defensible. If your grades are higher in your major, report the GPA for the major. If this year's grades are your highest, report the GPA for them. You need to know for sure whether or not there will be a GPA on the transcript your prospective employers get. If there will be, then you probably will want to include that GPA on your résumé, along with any other one that you calculate. That way you avoid looking as if you are trying to mislead an employer with sleight-of-hand GPA calculations.

How GPA Affects Employer Decisions

The first and probably the most important effect of GPAs on the recruiting process occurs when the decision is made to interview or not to interview you. This decision is based almost solely on résumé information, and will surely be made with less deliberation than later decisions that follow interviews. Once a prospective employer has begun to invest effort in you, they are likely to be more careful in weighing your strong and weak points.

> With the majority of employers, you are likely to be excluded from interviewing unless the GPA you report exceeds a cutoff. The cutoff varies between employers and may also vary between colleges. In most cases you won't know what this cutoff is.

Grades are important. Most companies use grades as the very first cutoff. The cutoff for some is 3.0 and for others it's 3.5. You'll have a very hard time getting your foot in the door if your GPA doesn't exceed the company's cutoff.

—Ryan Mossman, age 25

Other companies may cut off at 2.5, or at 2.0. The basic point is not that below some arbitrary number, you are dead. The point is simply that the higher the GPA, the richer the range of choices you will have.

The fact is that being good enough to stay in school or good enough to graduate or even good enough to get honors is not necessarily good enough to get the job offers you would like to have. This is true even if you went to a top college and have many accomplishments outside the classroom. It's true even if the job you want is not the most highly sought after job. There is no reliable substitute for GPA.

If you survive the cutoff for the first interview, the importance of GPA as a hiring criterion is likely to diminish as the employer gathers more information about you from the interview process and other documents. However, for each new interviewer, the GPA will leap out from the page as a prime element of résumé data, almost like an IQ. You may be asked to explain it or comment on it. You need to be ready to do so. Look ahead and try this task on for size. Fancying yourself a recruiter, how would you react to the following attempt to explain poor grades:

> *In some of those courses, the department limits the number of A's the instructor can give. And on our campus, somehow or other there hasn't been even one straight white male in our local honor organization, as far back as anyone remembers. That tells you something, doesn't it? So, I hope you won't hold my grades against me.*

Well, that's . . . plausible. But to you as a prospective employer, it sounds more like rationalization. So you write a note to yourself for later consideration that this fellow has a talent—for excuses. If you hire him to work on a project, he may end up delivering some very good excuses instead of the excellent results you need. Most companies prefer something closer to the military mode: "No excuse, sir." Employers want to hire winners, not whiners.

A high GPA says that you figured out how to do it, and you did it well. You should be expected to produce equal results after you graduate, even if the work environment and the tasks are quite different. To create such an expectation in your employer, you should go for a GPA that not only gets you past the cutoff, that is not only respectable and decent, but that knocks people's socks off.

How Much Is Enough?

You need to know how much you have to achieve in order to reach your goal. Psychologists confirm what common sense tells us, namely that people accomplish more when they are motivated by a concrete goal that is important to them. One such goal is getting chosen by the college you want, and another is getting chosen by the employer you want.

> *I didn't have to study in high school and neither of my parents went to college. In addition, I played on the varsity basketball and track teams and did work-study to finance my education. Grades were not my strong point. Many companies found my GPA of 2.7 worrisome. I didn't make it to the first round of interviews at some companies because of it. I still ended up in a great job that I enjoy, but my options upon graduation would have been much more numerous and varied had I buckled down and worked on that GPA.*

—*Sharon Spooler, age 25*

If you wait until you are a junior in college to find out how you need to perform in order to get the kind of job you want, then you may have waited too long. (But better late than never, and better somewhat late than terribly late.) Just as a proper balance of realism with hope is needed in applying to colleges, it's also needed in looking for jobs. There are many jobs and many employers, and for a lot of them GPA need not be decisive. Employers who need more candidates than they can readily find should be willing to look beyond your GPA. These can include companies in high-growth industries and industries that are unattractive to many students, as well as companies that don't make it easy for students to find them and apply. Other lines in your résumé can soften the impact of a low GPA.

In the most recent Employer Benchmark Survey conducted by the National Association of Colleges and Employers, in which 472 employers participated, work experience rated slightly above GPA as a factor used in prescreening college candidates. However, GPA was rated substantially above campus activities and other factors. If you're not strong on work experience, your GPA will be particularly crucial.

You may recall that in high school, nowhere could you readily find in print what kind of grades or rank in class you would need to get into colleges X and Y, though the facts were known. Well, in this book you are at least going to see something in print about how high a GPA is high enough:

> *Grades are probably the single most important factor in getting past the first cut. Keep your grades above a 3.5 if you can.*
>
> —*J.B. Mantz, age 25*

A 3.5 is halfway between an A and a B average, so it corresponds to getting half A's and half B's (or half A– and half B+ grades). That is as good a rough rule of thumb as any. A 3.0 GPA, a B average, is considered mediocre by many top firms. Begin aiming for A's, and wincing at A–'s.

During the recruiting process, I felt that my grades were given more importance than they should have been. Since I had a 3.14 GPA, it was sometimes difficult to convince potential employers to consider me.

—Marc Leferman, age 24

You know who you are. *You* know what you can do and what you have done already. But when a recruiter gets your résumé, all he knows about you is what he reads. He probably is not going to read everything you want him to read about you—or even your whole résumé—any more than you would read every word of every employment advertisement in the newspaper. So if you don't have top grades, you are inevitably going to think that your grades were given more importance than they should have been. But you can't keep that from happening, and you can't reverse it after it has happened. All you can do is make the sacrifices and compromises needed to get the GPA you need, so that at least the recruiters will invite you to the first interview and have a chance to see and hear who you really are.

My good grades got me a lot of interviews. It talked my way into the later rounds, too, and got plenty of offers. The thing that really shocked me was the companies' choice of the other students they interviewed. Many of these were people I knew hadn't done anything except go to class for four years. They weren't interesting, appealing people with fire, initiative, and leadership ability. They just went to class.

—Molly, age 23

Molly evidently found it insulting that the companies that appreciated her also appreciated others who, as she saw it, lacked some of her finest qualities. But no, Molly, those people did *not* just go to class. They went to class *and they got top grades.* That is why they excited broad and intense interest on the part of employers, even if their personalities were less than scintillating. How can an employer expect a person who did a less than first-rate job in college to do much better afterwards?

What every company needs and prefers to hire is first-rate employees, people with drive and potential. How can Avis expect to beat out Hertz if the people they hire are mediocre and uncompetitive? You may turn up your nose at McDonald's, but McDonald's has prospered and grown in highly varied environments and in the face of vigorous competition.

In business, competition is tough, the pace is accelerating, new answers are needed. Employers sense an intense need for winners, for people who are smart and who get what they want. Given the opportunity, they will choose to hire people who are resilient and adaptive—who can succeed with virtually any professor or any client. Not someone who is pretty good on average, but someone who is likely to get top marks on each assignment.

> Anyone can have a great résumé. I'm not looking for specific experiences. I'm looking for someone with a positive, "I can do anything if I put my mind to it" attitude.
>
> —Maritza Solari, Director of Medical Staff Services, California Pacific Medical Center

Ask a student with a 3.9 GPA what interviewers say about it. They quite honestly show that they are impressed. "How did you manage to do it?" some of them ask. Surely you can get the job without a 3.9, but the lower the GPA the harder it will be. If your GPA, taken together with your other qualifications, is too low to get you a spot on the interview list, then you won't have the opportunity to show what you can do, or to explain what you have done.

Apart from the GPA, almost everything else on a résumé is seen as soft and squishy, difficult or impossible to verify. The GPA and the college, rightly or wrongly, are generally read as uniquely "objective and quantitative" information—factual and subject to direct comparison between students. Your key challenge is to make the GPA work in your favor.

Students with GPAs of 2.0 or less get hired, of course. So do dropouts. But a 2.5 will make it easier and will open more choices for you than a 2.0. Whatever your GPA, you need to know how it relates to employer requirements, and what you can do to get the best offers that are within your reach.

I did poorly in college. My greatest interests were my fraternity and my dates. But I had friends and a family, and they helped me get a good job. What I regret is that I didn't learn how to buckle down and produce.

—Larry, age 62

Whether you did well or poorly relative to your classmates is not always obvious from your GPA. Colleges vary dramatically in their grading standards. At some highly selective colleges, more students get A's than B's, at least in advanced classes in subjects such as English and history. Almost no one flunks out. Yet, in some other colleges, the average freshman grade is as low as C, and many students flunk out. A recruiter on your campus will obviously make some allowances for these differences. Nonetheless, in the later part of the recruitment process, you will be competing against students from other schools. You can expect that GPA's will be compared with little if any allowance for differences in grading practices. In fact, the most recent Employer Benchmark Survey conducted by the National Association of Colleges and Employers showed that employers attach much more importance to GPA than to rank in class, even though the latter criterion eliminates any bias arising from divergent grading standards.

It's easy to feel that "an A from Harvard is worth more than an A from the local community college," but in many cases this might not be a fair reflection of the difficulty of getting these grades.

When it comes to finding a job, you are not going to be rewarded, or even compensated, for picking a college, a major, a course or a professor who grades low. Your GPA, all by itself, will be read as revealing whether you have been doing an excellent or a less-than-excellent job for four years. It puts you in a pigeonhole, where the recruiter equates you with others he has known (especially his own classmates) whose GPAs were approximately equal to yours.

Getting a Good GPA

If you want the best GPA you can get, the first thing you have to be is careful: careful not to take courses for which you are ill prepared, or for which the grading will be arbitrary or unduly harsh. Look for very small classes where the professor can feel affinity and even kinship because of your interest in his specialty. Many professors are honestly grateful for such attention, and it shows in their grades.

There is an opposing point of view:

I took the courses I wanted to take and learned what I wanted to learn. That's what college is for. I like the job I got, I have no regrets. My grades won't determine my future.

—Scott, age 22

You are going to learn much more after you get out of school than you ever learned before graduation. No one interviewed for this book disagrees with that statement. But after you finish university, you are somehow going to do your learning without the dubious benefit of exams and grades.

Learn whatever you want to learn in college, but make sure to keep an eye on the numbers that measure your learning. For example, if there's a great visiting professor on campus, go ahead and take the class . . . but think twice before enrolling for credit because his grading standards are almost surely unknown. This is much different from the way you are going to learn later on. Make sure your grades, like your activities and college jobs, help you rather than hurt you. Just make sure not to carry this thinking too far, because it's just as bad to believe that the only way you can learn is by getting a grade.

Of course, there will be tradeoffs for you to make. The least risky courses won't necessarily be the most interesting or the most useful ones. You will sometimes need to decide between "appearances" (GPA impact) and "substance" (inherent value to you of the course), based largely on how badly you need to maintain or enhance your GPA. You can play it safe by leaving the courses with the greatest grade risk until later in your college career, when you are likely to have stronger skills and more learning under your belt. If you leave a course until the last term of your senior year, it won't have any effect on the GPA you use while job hunting. This can be true even for courses taken in the first term of your senior year.

I took a full year course with a TA. Only the final grade counted. Towards the end of the year, the TAs went on strike for higher pay or something. I got a low grade for the year, and I couldn't even get to see my papers.

—Margot, age 21

What a distressing tale! But stories like these—genuine or not—can make you seem like a chump or a crybaby. Fact is, life is not fair and neither are grades. Somehow or other, though, despite all the randomness and unfairness, some people systematically do better than others, though not every single time. Remember that full-year courses and courses taught by TAs are risky, and you should avoid needless risks.

A fine story about grades is said to have happened at Harvard several decades ago. A student went in to see a famous professor to complain about a grade. The professor listened . . . and then punched him in the nose.

Well, many of us might well be willing to risk getting punched in the nose in order to have a reasonable chance of getting one of those "unfair" grades changed. But it would be wiser to avoid getting the bad grade in the first place by limiting your risks. Controlling risk requires forethought.

There is a "shopping period" at the start of each term. The incredible thing is that so few people, even among my friends, take advantage of it. They pick their courses from the catalog, and that's it. They may try to shuck a rotten TA, but they scarcely bother looking at other courses and they don't take advantage of the opportunity to leave their final choices until later in the term.

—Sandra, age 21

Depending on your school's flexibility, you can test your abilities and learn without taking big risks by auditing (which often enables you to take tests and do homework), by overenrolling and dropping the dud courses, or by bailing out of a course in which you are doing poorly. Or, you can make use of a credit/fail option. The same kind of flexible yet precise, goal-oriented thinking that you should apply to your academic program is what many employers want from you in doing your job.

> If your goal is learning, employers may have trouble seeing whether you attained it. What they are sure to see is your GPA.

The Credit/Fail Option

Many colleges offer you the option of taking a fraction of your courses on a credit/fail or similar ungraded basis. Check out your college's rules, in detail. This can be an excellent way to reduce risk, especially since it's usually possible to switch back to a letter grade even halfway through the term if you are doing well.

Students are sometimes reluctant to take courses credit/fail because it might not look good on their transcripts. However, the crucial decision to offer you a first interview will generally not be based on your transcript at all, but rather on your résumé and hence on your GPA. The company won't know how many classes you took credit/fail and isn't likely to care. How much mileage do you think you would get out of putting "Took no courses credit/fail" on your résumé? Not much.

Heck, I took some courses pass/fail. So did my friends. It's a way of trying something new without putting your whole record at risk.

Why on Earth would I hold it against someone I was recruiting, that they did the same thing I did?

—*Katherine, age 28*

Credit/fails may make it harder for you to get departmental or college-wide honors and be selected for honor societies such as Phi Beta Kappa, if you are a top student. However, little or none of this will happen until after you have your job and hence it won't affect your job hunt, though it may have some later significance if you plan to apply to graduate school. Look over the relevant rules and procedures and decide what is most important to you.

Choosing Your Courses

Some students worry that their GPA may be interpreted differently or downgraded on the basis of their choice of courses. They wonder whether an employer would prefer to see a fairly high GPA and a really tough choice of courses, as opposed to a top GPA and a lot of gut courses. In almost every instance, the right answer is "no." There are several reasons why the typical recruiter will go with your reported GPA number without trying to adjust it or apply it in a way that takes account of the difficulty or other characteristics of the courses you took.

First, in many situations the recruiter will only look at the résumé and not the transcript. The résumé is (let us hope!) lucid, while the transcript—if the recruiter gets one—will be full of obscure abbreviations and symbols. Of the two documents, the résumé is by far the more accessible and inviting.

*I look at the résumé as carefully as I can, and that loads me up for
the interview. On some campuses, the transcript is also in the book,
and I may glance at it. The courses and grades don't usually tell me
that much.*

—*Larry, age 27*

The individual who reads your file is unlikely to be in a good position to
rate the difficulty of your course program. To do this, she would have to
know about the workload and grading standards for hundreds of course
and instructors. In virtually every case, she doesn't know and doesn't care to
find out. She can't waste her time on trivia like that.

A recruiter's appreciation of your high GPA is unlikely to be
counterbalanced by contempt for the easy courses you chose, just as his
disrespect for your low GPA won't be much diluted by admiration for
the super-hard courses you attempted. The time to start thinking about
your GPA is when you pick your courses for your first college term. The
time to stop thinking about it is when you graduate. In between, you
will need to think about the GPA impact of any academic decision you
want to make.

Nondestructive Testing

If you want a high GPA, you need to find out quickly what courses you can
count on doing well in during the remainder of your college career. Then
you will at least have an opportunity and a choice, and if necessary you will
be able to decide later how to balance safety against interest. The courses in
which you get the best results without excessive effort in college won't

necessarily be in the same fields you found easiest in high school. One reason for this is that colleges offer many subjects that high schools don't.

> *In high school I loved English best of all. In college, I found other subjects such as art history and sociology, which I liked better, and where I could be surer of doing well. It's nice to find a field that's a little different and which people don't just follow their rut into.*
>
> —Ed, age 23

In trying a new field, there's no need to take a big risk by signing up for a full year course and leaving yourself no room to maneuver. You can shop carefully at the beginning of the term, going to the first meetings of more classes than you intend to take. Then you can either overenroll and thin down later, or you can enroll in the most desirable courses but audit others to hold open the possibility of making course changes later. If the workload is too tough or the prospect of a good grade too uncertain, or if the course seems useless or boring, you will then have a way out.

Equally important, make sure you are working from the best possible information. You can pay attention to student guides and reports, but they are not always reliable, particularly because instructors and courses change. Pay particular heed to what former students in the courses can tell you. Look at the exams, the papers, and the reading. Watch for year-to-year changes. Find out about the grading curve and the distribution of grades. Sometimes the registrar will divulge this information, or you can get it from the instructor himself. No information is 100 percent accurate as a projection of the future, but the more you know the better you can choose.

Personnel in key departments can be especially valuable information resources. These include the instructor who is responsible for undergraduate students and instruction (who at Yale is called the director of undergraduate studies, a rotating position), older undergraduate and graduate students, and even administrative assistants. After all, it's usually the administrative assistants who transmit the grade sheets, and many departments distribute grade statistics for all courses to their faculty to promote more consistent grading. You are looking for the courses and instructors with high percentages of A's, and you are particularly aiming to avoid situations in which high grades are scarce.

> When I asked, "Will I do better in this course or that course?" I always got a straight answer. Of course, it was a matter of opinion. But I'd rather have two or three expert opinions than a bunch of half-baked opinions.
>
> —Anne, age 24

Almost every department has get-togethers for students, even if these are primarily for graduate students. These may be coffees, or evening "club" meetings. Meet people and ask questions. You will quickly get the drift. Your primary purpose at such a gathering should be to become better informed and connected, rather than to find a lifetime companion. The more information you have, the better the decisions you can make.

Too Late?

It's never too late to work on your GPA. If you are not satisfied with your GPA after your sophomore year, it's not too late to salvage the situation. You still have time to improve your grades. The surest way to do this is to look at what you have done well at, and find more of the same—same instructor, similar subject matter, same format (term papers, or whatever). Avoid taking more courses for a grade than you can confidently handle.

Likewise, it's never too late to establish a context of activity in which your GPA may be judged more forgivingly.

The fact that I had been captain of the cheerleading team compensated for the fact that my grades weren't as good as some of the other candidates'. If you don't have top grades, interviewers want to know what you were doing with your time in college. If you were heavily involved in other activities, it may compensate for your academic performance.

—Eric Honeyman, age 24

In fact, whatever your grades, your capabilities will be seen in a more positive light if you are perceived as having spent a lot of your college time on other worthwhile activities. Whether you are a 4.0 or a 2.0, your academic performance is rated higher if it was achieved at the same time you were accomplishing other things.

Major Issues

Your major is potentially of major importance for just one reason. Like GPA, major is a handy abbreviation that sums up a lot of messy facts in a single word or number. A list of the courses you take would be lengthy. A description of their contents, often not obvious from their titles, would be far lengthier. The name of your major summarizes your courses in more or less the same way that your GPA summarizes your grades.

Grades have definite impact on a candidate's success in the recruiting process. But you should keep in mind that your education is a signaling device, and that courses you have taken are expected to reflect direction in your career. When I interview for my consulting firm, an English major with a 4.0 will be a much less compelling candidate than an engineering major with a 4.0 who has also taken courses in math and philosophy, for example.

—Andrew Ackerman, age 26

Andrew works for a consulting firm. Does this mean that consulting firms don't like English majors? No. What we can be sure of is that each evaluator has his own tastes, or biases, and these are triggered when he sees a candidate's major.

Your major need not box you in. You can explain your course work concisely and positively. "Took courses primarily in South American economics and politics." Or, "Course work focused on applying mathematical modeling techniques to physical problems." And every major is an "interdepartmental major" because it accepts at least a few courses in related disciplines, right? Employers like initiative. Show it in your choice of academic program.

With a little imagination, you can sum up your academic interests and experience in a phrase that is well adapted to your job goals. That is considerably better than having to look forward to dumb interview questions such as "And why are you interested in history? How do you think having studied history will help you succeed in our organization?" It's not too cool to say, "I just enjoy studying history" or, "Those are the courses I do the best in."

There are some kinds of jobs for which employers are looking for a specific major. Generally speaking, though, judging from the experiences of my peers, what you major in is of no importance. Employers care much more about whether you excelled in your major, what you did outside of class, and what you did during your summers.

—Michael Bernstein, age 24

Employers are ultimately interested in what you can do for them, secondarily in what you actually know that is relevant to the job, and only slightly in what you have studied. You will be targeting not only employers, but specific jobs. It's fine to be keenly interested in Intel or Yahoo! But you better think about what you want to do in your chosen company, and how you are going to show that you are ready to do it. Alternative ways of qualifying yourself include work experience, course work (not all of it necessarily in your regular terms and program of study, for grades), and what you can learn on your own.

Fewer than 30 percent of graduates interviewed for this book felt that their choice of major impaired their strength as job candidates, whereas more than twice as many regretted not having taken specific courses that would have been helpful in getting and succeeding in the first job.

Often, it's not obvious what an employer expects of a college graduate who, for example, wants to sell chemical products. But you can find out by asking for information. If the recruitment brochures don't tell enough, then ask more questions. It can't hurt. If the answers are vague, you should probably conclude that there are not very many specific requirements. Statements such as "We like to see a few courses in . . ." should be taken precisely at face value. If they say they prefer "chemical engineering majors," then get them to state what specific content they are looking for in such a major.

The point is that majoring in a particular field is often neither necessary nor sufficient to make sure that you have learned what your target employers want you to know. Make sure you can show that you know it. If the relevant courses might hurt your GPA, then find other ways to learn. With a little exploration and initiative, you can probably get approval for some independent study projects that fit your vocational needs better than the regular courses do. This is especially true if you are interested in a field that is developing and changing rapidly, such as computer design or programming.

When Major Conflicts with GPA

Often, the "best" or most prestigious major at your school is not the one in which you can get the highest GPA. This can happen because the major includes some required courses that are highly competitive, or that are taught by professors who are unlikely to give you A's.

On my campus, comparative literature is a tough and prestigious major, while literature is "for dilettantes." I was qualified for comparative literature, but I chose the other, to the consternation of the profs. As a result, I got a very high GPA, and the job offers I wanted. Not one interviewer had a clue as to the different majors, nor would they have cared.

—*Denise, age 23*

College is a little world of its own, even if it's located in a city and in no way walled off from the noncollege world. At your college, some majors may be open to a limited number of students or may have difficult prerequisites. These may carry prestige within the college. All the more so, perhaps, if the hardy souls who enter such a major do so at the likely sacrifice of their GPA's, because the grading in the major is tough.

The problem for you is that these attitudes lose their relevance at the exit to the campus. The same decisions and results that are rewarded at college may be punished by the outside world of employment. Face forward by making the choices that will be rewarded. This may mean considering a less prestigious major—a decision that affects you only in the short run. If you don't particularly care what you major in—say, history, classics, philosophy, and English all sound fine to you—then pick the major you think you will do best in. But some scientific and technical career paths won't allow much latitude in major selection. If you want to build bridges, for example, you have to major in civil engineering. If you want to design rockets, you have to major in physics. If you choose to pursue a competitive, difficult course of study, be prepared to buckle down and fight hard for your GPA.

Must I Take Accounting?
Or . . . What?

6

From the time you enter college, it's important to have some view of what you want to do after college. Experience relevant to the field in which you are interested will affect your ability to successfully interact with recruiters.

—*Eric Zausner, former partner at Booz, Allen & Hamilton*

What is recommended in the quote is "experience relevant to the field." This experience can include internships and activities on the campus. The courses you take for credit constitute a significant part of your college experience, and of your qualifications for employment. Once you have job targets in mind, you will want to make sure that your program includes any courses demanded or desired by employers who hire for these jobs. Alternatively, you need to be able to satisfy these employers that you have gained the requisite skills in some other way.

The ultimate authority on your classes and grades—and on almost nothing else—is your transcript. It will say exactly which courses you have taken at college for credit. If you have also taken courses elsewhere (for instance, in summer school or even by correspondence), or have passed external examinations such as the Advanced Placement tests, you will have transcripts for these also.

Your transcripts generally won't be looked at in detail when a decision is made by an employer about giving you a first interview. Your résumé may, if you wish, refer to particular subjects you have studied or examinations you have passed. Failure to mention a subject on your résumé would not imply that you have not studied it. If your major, as described in the résumé, doesn't obviously fit the needs of the job, your résumé can also include a brief and general reference to other relevant learning. For instance: "Course concentration in psychology. Other subjects studied have included accounting, statistics, and computer science."

> *I majored in international studies. My résumé highlighted the business relevance. And interviewers challenged me to show that I had consciously been looking towards an international business career.*
>
> —*Robin, age 23*

It is in your interviews that you will be able to explain, or will be asked to show, what you know and how you learned it. Through the interview process, you will need to satisfy employers that you are qualified for the jobs they offer. Though job requirements vary, it's worth considering some of the questions that are most likely to arise.

Over half the graduates interviewed for this book felt that the key issue they faced in interviewing was their quantitative training and capabilities.

Some Words About Numbers

Before focusing on any skills as specific as those of accounting, many employers want to see that you are comfortable with numbers and with quantitative methods of analysis. If your college work has been primarily in nonquantitative fields (these range from English to biology), you can expect to be challenged. "They stopped making me take math in tenth grade. Thank goodness!" is not a response that is effective with interviewers.

> *In the later interviews, a couple of them said, "I don't see anything quantitative here." I answered "Well, I got a 5 in the AP Calculus BC exam," and that was all they needed to hear.*

> *—Beth, age 22*

Good for Beth! But, suppose you really did stop taking math in tenth grade—then what?

Every job, even if it's not strictly a "business" job, involves your being paid. In other words, it involves numbers and exists within the context of an economy driven by concepts of financial value and profit. Even if you are so literary that publishers race to interview you, your future in editorial work is dim if you can't master or have no interest in the rudiments of how books or magazines make money. Interviewers will see that. You're welcome to like or dislike this situation, but you're not going to change it.

There is more, but you already know it. The quantitative people, who are now a ruling majority, harbor attitudes towards the visibly nonquantitative that can range from bare tolerance to ill-concealed contempt. Mark Twain became a steamboat captain (before becoming an author) without knowing or caring about numbers, but that's not likely today.

If you detest numbers, it won't pay either to revel in what you are or to try to change it. What you need is cosmetics, not surgery. Look quantitative enough, identify with the quantitative. It doesn't have to go more than skin deep to help you get hired.

As I rose in management, I found that there were some "numbers guys" at all levels, but most of the key managers are less analytical and more people oriented. Sure, you need to be able to read accounting reports and have a grounding in finance, but we couldn't learn that in college anyway.

—*Ella, age 34*

In other words, it will be wise for you to try to emulate Beth's result (that is, to satisfy interviewers that you are sufficiently quantitative) without imitating her method (taking calculus and doing well in it). Sure, calculus is the typical first-year, college-level math course. Sure, lots of people take it. And sure, it's "graded hard." But getting an A in calculus won't make you any better at doing most jobs, and getting a low grade may keep you from getting the job in the first place. Thus, if you're not planning to be a scientist or if you're no good in math, then why take calculus for a grade? If you feel a burning need to learn it, you can take a correspondence course or learn it on your own or audit the class. Better yet, study it after you retire.

I struggled through calculus and did all right, but it distracted me from all my other courses and really wrecked my year. In the ten years since then, I've never had any use for anything I learned in that course, although I use numbers all the time in my work as a financial analyst.

—*Beverly, age 32*

If you don't like theorems and variables, find something other than calculus that is quantitative enough for employers and not too much for you to handle. The course catalog is one place to look. If your college has a math or similar requirement, then you need to see how to meet this requirement with minimum risk of jeopardizing your GPA and your transcript. There may be computer, history of science, or other courses that enable you to satisfy the quantitative requirement without really doing anything quantitative. That may not be enough by itself to satisfy employers, but at least it should protect your GPA.

An introductory course in statistics may be a good way to show that you can handle numbers. Such courses are often given in social science departments such as psychology. They are less theoretical than calculus, and much more likely to be useful to nonscientists. Facility with statistics is a marketable skill for jobs in many business fields, ranging from marketing to quality control.

You don't have to take courses for grades at your college in order to satisfy employers about your numeracy. How does this sound: "While in college, I tutored high school students in math and coached their math team. It was very satisfying, and it deepened my own understanding." Of course, you need some details to back that up! Or, "I worked evenings at H&R Block for several months. It's really fun saving people money on their taxes!" (Do not be surprised if the interviewer asks for your help with his own tax problems.) As a last resort, find something academic but slightly exotic. It will give you an excuse for getting outside the standard, and highly competitive, math curriculum. "I wanted to apply specialized statistical techniques to my research on voting patterns, so I went to a summer workshop at Oklahoma State." Or, "I took a course in economic history where I learned and applied techniques of input-output analysis."

There was a course in the economics department that counted as
quantitative, but it actually involved discussion of business cases. I
wangled my way in without the elementary Ec. That was the most
useful course I took, and it even helped me with my interviews.

—*Petra, age 26*

Computer Courses

You are practically certain to need some computer skills in your first and subsequent jobs. You are not likely to need to know how to program in complex object languages such as C++ (although that is one of the fastest growing fields of work, and one of the easiest in which to get a job). Nor will you need to be a professional in computer science, a field that is for mathematicians or engineers. What you need to be able to do is to use the computer as a work tool.

Take a computer class. If you've got no computer skills, your first
job is going to be an uphill battle.

—*Billy May, age 27*

Perhaps it has always been this way. If you are fluent in the dominant technology of your generation, you have a big advantage.

An old man once got fed up with home when he was a kid and came to New York to make his fortune—without a college degree, naturally. He was a self-directed type, not at all the kind of person who would be interested in competing for a high GPA. At that time the typewriter was a rarity, as were people who could operate one. Typing was a high-powered career, reserved for men only. Sales of typewriters were limited by the number of people trained to operate them. This fellow walked in off the street to a typewriter manufacturer's storefront, and proceeded to learn to type there. That was all he needed to earn a nice living, and he moved up from there, eventually going into advertising.

That may seem like ancient history, but the reason it's relevant is that precisely the same kind of opportunities exist today. If you know Hypertext Markup Language (HTML), a super-simple language used in constructing Web sites, then you can be in demand at $40,000 per year. Not a fortune, but compared with being a bank teller or even teaching school, it's not a bad start. And you can work almost anywhere. Nobody will ask you whether you went to college, much less what you majored in, much less your GPA—except out of idle curiosity. It is, however, a good example of how technology can rapidly generate demand for specific job skills. Move towards the opportunities.

You don't have to learn HTML, but if your last term paper wasn't written on a computer or if you are not communicating with distant friends by e-mail—then you are part of a vanishing species. You are also missing a lot that could make your life easier, more flexible, and more pleasant. If you think it's too expensive to use computer power, then you are out of touch with the facts. If you think it's too hard to learn how, then you are positioning yourself a continent away from the job market. The fact that your parents or other older people you know protest that they can survive without much use of computers shows only that as the world changes around them, they have managed to find a niche that, for the moment, is protected. This is not an example you should follow.

I wish I had taken a few computer classes and gained some basic computing skills during my college years.

—*James, age 29*

The more work you can do on a computer, including communications, the more efficient and desirable you will be as a worker. To learn how, talk to your friends. If they can't give you the advice you need, then hightail it to your campus computer center, learn what you need, buy it, and get up to date. The best fringe benefit your college offers may well be not the dining hall or the health center, but the access to computer resources, including advice and training.

This is true particularly because computer system capabilities have far outrun documentation, at least the official documentation provided by manufacturers. Helpful books are available, starting with the *For Dummies* series, as in *The Internet for Dummies*. However, the most prevalent mode of learning about computers is by doing, as well as from friends or co-workers. Today's systems don't blow up because you pushed the wrong button. Practice makes perfect.

Almost every college offers one or two baby courses, for credit, that amount to "how to use a computer"—imparting skills such as word processing, creation of an Internet home page, and the like. Learn to do all those things first, outside the class. Then take the courses for easy A's. You may find you like this stuff, and you may go on to additional course work that focuses on skill building and projects rather than on memorization and exams. The more you can learn that is practical, such as computer graphic design, the better.

With or without the benefit of courses, you should know not only word processing, but database and presentation systems, such as those included in Microsoft Office. These skills are highly likely to be helpful in any career you enter.

Even interviewing for internships, they would ask me, "What systems do you know how to use?" Intimidating question! But simple answers are fine. And you should be able to do word processing, spreadsheets, presentations, and navigation on the Internet.

—*Nick, age 24*

While many universities have mostly Macintosh computers, the great majority of businesses rely on PC's. For word processing and spreadsheets, it's fairly easy to move from Macintosh to PC's. But if you are going to be doing anything more complicated, you should learn to do it on a PC.

Accounting

"Accounting is for accountants," right? And you certainly have no interest in becoming an accountant, so why learn any accounting?

All too often, young people pursue certain careers because they think they will ensure their financial security. I have tons of friends who were accounting majors and are unhappy with their jobs and choice of career.

—*Billy May, age 27*

That's one man's opinion, and it's surely shared by others. But most people who take introductory accounting courses won't become accountants, and the great majority of these people find accounting useful.

> Only 17 percent of graduates surveyed for this book who had taken a course in accounting felt that it was a waste of their time.

Accounting is sometimes referred to as the language of business. It is accounting that tells you whether your business is making a profit or going broke. You won't be able to work that out just by looking at your bank account.

Accounting is often the only course offered by liberal arts colleges that gives an employer the clear signal that you have consciously and intelligently committed to a business career. Failure to learn accounting can be a serious disadvantage.

> *As I got closer to the final round of interviews, employers kept questioning whether I had made a knowledgeable decision to pursue business. I wound up with just one really good job offer. That employer, to my amazement, said as a condition of the job that they would have a tutor come to my office weekly to teach me accounting.*
>
> —*Daniel, age 25*

Quite a few liberal arts colleges offer just one obscure accounting course, disdained by the economics department and counting towards no major. It may be hard to find that course in your catalog, but you should at least audit it, unless you choose to learn your accounting somewhere else, or by correspondence.

This is not only about getting a job. There are a great many things you can learn on the job, but unlike many of those things, accounting is a coherent discipline that is best tackled holistically, rather than one random piece at a time. Whatever job you get will focus on objectives and results, and these should tie to accounting numbers.

Economics

For reasons that are somewhat elusive, economics is widely regarded as the "liberal arts" discipline that is most closely related to business. After all, economics has to do with buying and selling, and so does business. So, as chemistry and biology are to medicine, economics is to business, more or less.

Would-be medical students flood the elementary chem courses, where they compete desperately for the good grades indispensable for medical school admission. Well, at least these people have the justification that two full chem courses are a minimum requirement for applying to medical school. However, economics is not generally required either for admission to business school or for business jobs. If you think that economics courses are needed for what you want to do after college, check this out carefully.

> Everyone said, "If you're going into business, take economics." I really don't know why they said that. At most, ten percent of what I studied has come up in my work. It surely wasn't worth it, and it wasn't fun or easy.
>
> —Timothy, age 30

Economics is not an exception. If you are going to take a course that is not required for the jobs you want or for graduate school, then make sure it's not going to hurt your GPA.

Education for Business

Some universities make it possible for undergraduates to major in business or in a field of business such as marketing, or to spend their last two college years primarily in business courses. These schools include the University of Pennsylvania (Wharton), University of Virginia, and University of California—Berkeley. Liberal arts colleges generally don't offer this opportunity.

Because the most prestigious and best endowed American institutions—including most of the Ivies—shun undergraduate education for business, the basic concept of undergraduate education for business lacks the backing of educational opinion leaders. It is afflicted with the taint of "trade schools," for-profit education, and (horrors!) night school. It may not be fair, but if you study business as an undergraduate, some employers may stigmatize you, often silently, as narrow and uncultured. This is one more reason many students reject the idea of studying business at the undergraduate level, even though many students who do study business as undergraduates are well prepared for work and students who take no business courses often feel lost:

> When I started work, I found there were these people who had studied business as undergraduates. How I envied them! They seemed to know what it all meant. But I caught up.
>
> —Irene, age 27

Hence, the most desirable compromise, unavailable to many, is to stick with a liberal arts major but cross-register in order to take a number of basic business courses including accounting from a good business faculty. When it's feasible, this strategy gives you the best of both worlds. You will have a strong head start when you go to work—and a real advantage if you go to business school later—but you won't be tarred as not really having gone to college. By picking your business courses selectively, you can also avoid the intense grade competition typical of undergraduate business majors.

Foreign Languages

Languages are among the minority of nontechnical college courses that have potential direct application to work, particularly if you are interested in international opportunities in any field. Continuing globalization enhances this value. Some companies emphasize identifying "exportable" managers and gives such managers special prominence.

> *I wish I had focused more on developing competence in a foreign language. Mobil wants to transport its star junior members to work in their offices in developing markets. Without the language competence, I simply can't compete for those positions and I feel that I am at a disadvantage because of it. Fluency in another language will give you an edge far and above equally qualified people when interviewing at Mobil.*
>
> —*Eric Honeyman, age 24*

Some feel that the career advantages of language competence go beyond the particular needs and preferences of international companies.

The foreign dimension is a vital component of a successful career. By gaining work experience abroad or learning a foreign language well enough to survive in that country while in college, you will be ahead the game.

—Bob Taylor, former director of the lab at Digital Equipment Corporation, which was one of the pioneers in developing the Internet

If you start from zero, to acquire a level of oral competence in a foreign language that is useful for business purposes will require at least three full years of college study, though some colleges offer accelerated courses for double credit that can speed this process. Opinions differ as to whether college is the right place to learn a new language, and as to whether language study is an optimal use of your time in the college classroom. How you choose to pick up this important skill is up to you.

Other Relevant Courses

A number of interviewees had taken other courses, not explicitly related to business, that they had found helpful in getting and doing their jobs. Psychology is one such field.

The sociology and psychology courses I took in college have served me to this day. It was in these courses that I learned about how to motivate people to get the job done and how to work constructively with others.

—Maritza Solari, Director of Medical Staff Services, California Pacific Medical Center

The logic of this is clear, but experiences differ. Few employers specifically look for this kind of background, but the understanding gained from sociology and psychology courses might certainly be valuable to you in your job. While business schools teach about organizational behavior, they don't require psychology or sociology courses as prerequisites. If courses with clearly job-relevant content have more general or theoretical courses as prerequisites, it can be particularly difficult to see whether the investment of effort will have long-term justification.

Coursework that enhances communications skills is also cited as a source of on-the-job effectiveness.

The course I took in public speaking has been invaluable to me in providing me with basic skills I need to make presentations.

—*Billy May, age 27*

> Not all jobs focus on formal presentations, but the great majority require the ability to inform and persuade orally.

Taking a course in public speaking may be a good choice for you. However, a college course is not the only way to learn public speaking. Debating is another way. Neither debating nor a public speaking course necessarily focuses on the skills most crucial to oral business communication. These skills include the ability to understand the motives and goals of others, and to inspire them to commitment and action.

Skills in written communication are very important in some jobs, but relatively unimportant in many others. Now that E-mail is here to stay, however, even people whose job descriptions don't include writing need to

have the ability at the very least to express themselves clearly in short written messages. The inability to form a coherent paragraph reflects poorly on an employee, no matter what her function or title. Some interviewees felt that the writing they did in college classes was of great help in preparing them to be effective writers in the business setting.

> *The ability to write clearly and persuasively is the most important skill I need for my job. Ninety percent of what I do is writing to others at the firm and telling them about my findings and insights.*
>
> —*John, age 25*

You can also improve your writing by working on student publications, through research or tutorial courses, or in part-time jobs and internships.

What About Grad School?

In many fields, both business and technical, you can expect to be competing down the road with people who have graduate degrees. For the major professions such as law and engineering, graduate education is virtually a necessity. Decisions about graduate school are serious.

> *If you wish to pursue a career in computing, you will face a major decision upon graduation. Will you go out into the field with just a B.S. or will you get a graduate degree? Your decision will make quite a difference in where you end up 20 years down the road. That's why it's important to seek guidance from professors and contacts in the industry.*
>
> *—Roy Levin, Director, Systems Research Center, Digital Equipment Corporation*

Yes, there's a major decision to be made before graduation by students who could go on straight from college to graduate school. But put this decision in perspective. You are not deciding while in college whether you will ever go to graduate school. If you decide not to go now, you can always decide to go back later on.

On the other hand, if you go directly from college to graduate work and later change your career direction, the extra training won't necessarily help you. Although employers are quite liberal in accepting the peculiar interests that you nourished in college, a wrong educational move after college can detract from your credibility by making you look like a dilettante.

> Going to graduate school is not the right move unless and until you are quite confident of the direction of your career, and the relevance of your graduate study to that career.

The decision that has to be made in college is only whether your immediate goal at graduation will be graduate school admission or a job. If you're not sure yet, then you need to inform yourself about the requirements of both employers and graduate schools, work towards a decision between them, and meanwhile try to build a record that will hold your options open. You may want to apply both to graduate schools and for jobs, even if you're already virtually sure of what you want to do. This can help you get a measure of your acceptability both for employment and for further education.

I applied to business and law school, and also for jobs. One business school admitted me with a one-year delay. Two law schools admitted me, and I deferred the one I liked best. But I wound up taking a job. I'm looking forward to working!

—Helen, age 22

Decades ago, the common conception was that at least if you have enough money to pay for it, your education should run continuously until it ends forever. Taking a couple of years off between college and business school was thought to make about as much sense as doing so after two years of high school, or after two years of medical school—namely, no sense at all—unless the delay was a financial necessity.

> *When I went to college, you either got a job with limited prospects right away, or else you went straight for an M.B.A. that would qualify you for much more pay and the interesting jobs in the prestige companies. All that has changed. The most selective M.B.A. programs won't take you out of college, but some of the most desirable employers will take you for two or three years until you go to business school.*

—Ron, age 58

The economic logic of the old system was clear. You are worth much more money after you finish your education, therefore you lose money by stopping to work before you finish. That is still true. But now some other considerations are given weight. One of these is that you may have a better idea of what, if anything, you want to study further if you have had some practical experience after college and before committing yourself to further education.

That sounds logical too. But when almost all students went straight from college to medical school, very few dropped out of medical school, or out of the medical profession later. This was true despite the fact that both medical school and subsequent training were considerably more gruesome than they are now, and interns and residents were paid far less. The same is broadly true of law school, and of business school.

The transition to deferral of graduate education, particularly business education, probably wasn't aimed primarily at encouraging people to make more mature and stable choices of career. In the case of the business schools, it was the schools themselves, more specifically the most selective of them, who took the initiative. They first discouraged and then largely ruled out applicants who proposed to come straight from college. The reason given by the schools is that students who have practical experience get more out of their business education. They are better students and the instruction and class discussion can proceed at a higher level, with students learning much more from each other.

> *Work for two years before going back to graduate school. When I taught at Stanford, I found that students who had worked for a year or two before returning to school were much more motivated and focused than those who had come straight out of college.*
>
> *—Dr. Vinton Cerf, Senior Vice President, Internet Architecture and Engineering, MCI*

From the individual point of view, a different answer may be the right one.

> *I got into Harvard Business School right out of college. Their catalog said they wanted at least two years of experience, but I got in. It gave me a tremendous head start, I've never regretted it.*
>
> *—Marlene, age 31*

Will Going to Business School Make You Much More Valuable?

Even 10 years ago, the new pattern of working for a few years before going to business school was firmly established:

> *I graduated and got a job in marketing at American Express. I wanted to go to Harvard Business School, and they obviously wouldn't take me without job experience. After two years, they did accept me. Although my employer hadn't offered to pay for business school, when I graduated they rehired me with a big promotion and raise.*

> —*Susan, age 36*

At first glance, it may seem strange that American Express found Susan enormously more valuable after two years at Harvard Business School than she had been immediately before. She didn't feel all that much more competent or effective! But the difference wasn't in Susan's anticipated contribution to the enterprise. That would be hard to estimate in any case. What had changed so drastically was Susan's market value.

Our generation has been brought up to believe that markets are well-nigh infallible. There may be occasional minor imperfections, but we can count on the invisible hand of the market to smooth them over very quickly. So, where there's smoke there's very likely fire. If Harvard Business School almost doubled Susan's market value, then where is the "real" value that is (almost surely) being reflected in that market value?

Several factors might contribute to Susan's rapid increase in value while at Harvard. First, maybe going to Harvard actually inculcates the secrets of success, or at least some bundle of skills and resources that makes people more effective and valuable. Interviewees saw it differently.

> *The most important thing I got out of business school, apart from the degree and the hiring process, was the interaction with fellow students, who came with all different experiences and perspectives. They will be helpful later in my career, too.*

—*Tony, age 29*

After two years at a good business school you can expect to have some contacts that will be valuable to you later. But those contacts are unlikely to be of a nature that would add to your value to an employer such as American Express. They would be more likely to reduce your value, by making it more likely that you would soon receive job offers at higher pay, so that the employer would either have to pay up or let you go.

A selective business school may also add to your market value by dint of the selection process from which you emerged victorious. If lots of people think that a particular business school is number 1 or even number 5, then they will want to go there. The school gets its pick, and the people it chooses are supposed to be the best. So, if you earn a degree from one of these schools, that fact labels you as the cream of the crop.

> *I wanted to go straight from college to an M.B.A. It was only after I was halfway through the program that I happened to see an article that showed that the average pay people get when they graduate here is only about 60 percent as much as at a few other schools. That's not all due to the fact that many of us are younger!*

—*Arthur, age 24*

The aspiring student, if he's smart, takes experiences like this to heart and looks at a published table that compares, among other things, the average pay received by people graduating from each school. These tables depend almost entirely on unverified data provided by the schools themselves (and ultimately on data provided by the graduating students), so they are by no means fully reliable. Surely, there must be some schools that are on the way up (or even on the way down), where current starting salary levels are a lagging indicator of value. But the information in the table is much better than nothing. With this data in hand, how would you go about making the tradeoff between pay, on the one hand, and the theoretical value you would personally assign to the education, on the other hand?

The reported differences in pay levels between schools remain huge. In minor part, these differences are misleading. If you find a good table, it will also show the average age of the graduates. (Age information can also be found in the catalogues of the schools.) Obviously, older students have more work experience and were earning more than younger ones immediately before they went to business school. Hence they will tend to be employed at higher salaries afterwards. Similarly, people with a particular work background, such as consulting or engineering, will tend to have been earning more and hence to continue earning more. But most of the differences in average pay derive from the market value that the schools impart to their graduates, in part through the selection process.

More so than for a college degree, the market value of an M.B.A. depends in part on where you are in your career, but even more on the where you get that M.B.A. Rushing to get an M.B.A. from a less-than-well-known business school will make less sense than waiting and doing your best to get admitted to one of the most selective schools. But for any particular school, it will be to your advantage to go ahead and get your degree as early as possible—even right after college if that possibility is available, which it very seldom is. If the school you want, the most selective of the schools you are ever likely to be able to attend, might take you now, then go ahead and apply, and plan on attending if admitted.

Of course, these guidelines don't apply to all possible situations.

> *I went from the university to a major consulting firm. After two years, they offered to pay for my business school, but suggested that I skip that and accept right away the same promotion I would be offered after the M.B.A. I accepted that offer, but after a year I left to work in venture capital, where I had a better opportunity to create value.*
>
> *—Mike, age 26*

This is exceptional rather than normal. Perhaps the firm felt that without an M.B.A., Mike would be less likely to receive and accept an offer from another employer. That is good for them, but possibly bad for Mike, who would have less chance to make employers bid for him.

Overall, Mike saved time and made more money by skipping the M.B.A. However, he had to compare the immediate advantages of accepting the offer against whatever he thought the M.B.A. might be worth to him later in his career. This longterm aspect is worth considering.

What Is an M.B.A. Worth to You in the Long Run?

Three years from now, when a prospective employer is considering offering you a 20 percent raise to jump ship, a prestigious M.B.A. might loom large on your résumé, confirming your desirability and value. This would be the case particularly if the prospective new employer could not easily get references or even confirm your current compensation, because you have not yet left your present job. Human resources people and senior management, who have not met you, might be more willing to approve your hiring if they saw objective proof of your standing. Even your then-current employer might be willing to give you a larger raise because of your stronger résumé. However, the M.B.A. is by no means the only measure of high value in a business person.

> We're not good at bringing in senior people from other companies, so we have to grow them. After someone has been here five years, we all know him. The most promising guy we have is still under thirty. He happens to have an Engineering M.A., but it wouldn't matter whether he had a Harvard M.B.A., a Ph.D., or nothing. He's just the best.
>
> —Bruce, Senior VP, Human Resources, Fortune 500 Company

Thirty years from now, when the CEO is considering anointing you, or your rival, as her successor, she's scarcely likely to give much weight to whether or not you have an M.B.A., or where you got it. She will focus on your more recent accomplishments, and even more on your qualities as an executive and as a person. At that point, the M.B.A. is not going to render you a whole lot more credible to constituencies such as directors and securities analysts. It's unlikely to make a bit of difference in your compensation, either.

But it's a long way from here to your position 30 years out. Along the way, you might get derailed, and find yourself urgently looking for a job under circumstances in which credentials count for more than personal contacts and claims of accomplishment. At that point, the M.B.A., particularly if it's from a respected school, could make a significant and very beneficial difference, providing a form of partial unemployment insurance. But it can never provide a guarantee that you will get the kind of employment you want, or even any employment at all.

Normally, the farther you go in your career, the less your distant past credentials matter. It's a case of "What have you done lately?" In fact, given two people of roughly equal and substantial proven accomplishment, some observers will be inclined to attribute greater talent to the one who has succeeded despite having fewer advantages, including educational advantages such as an M.B.A. And there have always been managers and others who look on M.B.A.s as a group with negative feelings that range from skepticism to envy to open hostility. You will need to be very sensitive to this.

> The new CEO brought in a bunch of M.B.A.'s as well as consultants. They were going to teach us marketing. Guess what? None of it worked. They are all gone, and our marketing hasn't changed.

—Dave, age 53

As a credential, the M.B.A. on average does more good than harm, but it does some harm as well as a larger amount of good. This leaves for last the question of whether or how or to what extent the M.B.A. will actually make you a more effective manager, rather than merely a more sought after and highly paid one. After all, the choice is not between business school and two years of sleep. The choice is between business school and two years of work experience, and that experience would also add to your skills. Business school is better planned and more systematic, but it's not as practical.

> *The most practical thing about business school was that unlike my earlier education, we did a lot of the work in groups or teams, and this functioned well. You learn how to focus, specialize, listen, compromise, and put results ahead of ego.*

—*Annie, age 29*

> *Was business school worth it? Well, put it this way. It was more fun than working, and it made my pay go up faster. I never calculated the return on investment, but I'm glad it's on my résumé.*

Steve, age 31

Only 12 percent of business school graduates who were interviewed for this book question whether the M.B.A. was worth the money and effort it cost.

A good M.B.A. can also have very important indirectly favorable effects on your career by making you more confident as you articulate your views, make decisions, and compete with others for advancement.

> *I studied math and computer science in college, after which I got a programming job and later a marketing and management job. I learned a lot and rose to become a senior vice president, but I never felt comfortable that I understood "business," and particularly finance. I think I've reached my limit.*

—*Jane, age 43*

Why is it that Jane didn't get her M.B.A. at some early point in her career? For one thing, she had not particularly liked being a student, and she had particularly disliked her college. She had never seen much connection between what she had studied and what she needed to do in her job, and had started work without any particular career orientation. For all these reasons, the idea of giving up her position (in a company where M.B.A.'s were not particularly prized), going back to school, and enduring two more years of classes was never appealing.

Over the course of 20 years, the situation had evolved. Increasingly, Jane was working shoulder to shoulder with, or competing against, people who regarded themselves as professional managers, a status she had never sought or claimed for herself. Intellectually, she was surely capable of learning whatever she needed to know on her own, or by taking a couple of courses. But she never did it; she was intimidated. When she made big mistakes (as every manager does from time to time), she wondered whether they resulted from ignorance, from lack of education. Probably, her company should have sent her (somewhat against her will, most likely) to one of the three- to six-month, middle-management programs offered by leading business schools. There, she would have seen that her intelligence, objectivity, insights, and experience gave her a relative advantage over the majority of executives at her level, assembled from across a broad spectrum of companies.

How What You Do in College Can Affect Your Admission to Business School

We have seen that if you wind up going to business school, then getting into the best school you can will be very important, and getting into that school sooner rather than later can also be important. Of course, you may not know about whether or when you are going to business school until you get your job offers, and see how your opportunities lay out, But because there's a significant possibility that if you want a business career you will want business school, the decisions you make while in college need to take account of that possibility.

> *If you're going to work, I don't care if it's in government, charity, medical, law—business school can't hurt you. It's really the only training that is relatively universal. And now some schools are offering an M.B.A. in just a little over a year. That is worth considering.*

> *—Patty, age 26*

The decisions that affect your attractiveness to business schools are not primarily decisions about courses. Business schools, like law schools, tend not to impose specific course requirements for admission. They are even more unlikely than are employers to pick through your transcript course by course to judge the difficulty or relevance of your program. But, you have to show them that you know what business is about. For this, your job decisions are crucial. Successful, preferably high profile internships or other work experience count for more than any specific course work in demonstrating commitment and adaptation to a business career. Likewise, recommendations from professors, except for those who are nationally distinguished, are likely to count less than recommendations from employers.

Business schools ask for a recommendation from a former professor, so if that is something you might be interested in pursuing, you need to develop a mentoring relationship with at least one professor. A friend of mine took a course by Paul Volcker, former chairman of the Federal Reserve. Paul Volcker then wrote recommendations for his job and business school applications.

—Michael Avila, age 29,

In one respect, business school admissions is very similar both to college admissions and to law and medical school admissions: Business school admissions is strongly driven by test scores, in this case by GMAT scores. These scores furnish the only criterion that can impartially rank all candidates. This makes the scores very easy to use as selection criteria and largely accounts for their importance.

Your GPA (or rank in class) and your college—as well as your work experience—also count for quite a lot in the business school admissions competition. But, which is easier for you to improve—your GPA, your work record, or your GMAT score? For most people, it's their GMAT score. After all, your GPA is set in stone and you can't change your career overnight. Therefore, be very thorough and diligent in your preparation for the GMAT, and to avoid taking the test for the record until you are highly confident of doing very well on it. Schools will see every score you put on your record, whatever they may say about counting only the highest of them.

You may find it worthwhile to take a test-prep class for the GMAT like those offered by Kaplan. The best time to take the test itself is when you can focus all your attention on it during the preceding 6–8 weeks. Take the test seriously: The business schools do. And no score except your highest can be confidently counted as good enough.

I got a GMAT book and glanced at it. There didn't seem to be anything I needed to study, so I went and took the test. That was a mistake.

—Karen, age 24

Specialized Business Training

There are a number of alternatives to the standard, broad gauge M.B.A. program that may merit consideration in individual cases. These are aimed at specific and narrower career paths, but the choice of one of these paths won't necessarily render you ineligible to rise to a high position in a large organization.

For instance, some universities offer course programs that can prepare you for the state examinations for the Certified Public Accountant credential while also giving degree credit. The CPA credential is essential only if you want to open an accounting practice or do audit work for a public accounting firm. Some of the largest and highest paying of these firms, such as Arthur Andersen, have shown far more growth in nonaccounting fields such as consulting than in accounting in recent years.

Being a CPA with some audit experience in a large firm remains a good route towards corporate accounting and financial jobs. These can lead to your becoming a chief financial officer (CFO). Some CFOs, including accountants, rise to become CEOs. If you are numbers oriented, the CPA route may help you circumvent much of the competition and jump you to a good corporate job with considerable professional content.

I went to State, studied accounting, and worked part time. Then, I got a job as junior auditor with Ernst & Young, one of the biggest.

*After becoming a manager there, I was hired away by a client,
which is very common. So, I became controller of a small company.
It grew fast, and I'm now the CFO. I'll never run the company, but
I've done a lot with what I've got.*

—Peter, age 36

Peter doesn't have an M.B.A., but his work is interesting and respected, and
his professional credentials help to support his market value. To many of
the nonfinancial managers he works with, Peter personifies indispensable
financial and accounting lore, and he dispenses it authoritatively. Not a bad
position to be in. If Peter is not going to rise any higher, that will be because
of lack of desire or self-confidence, not because his company views him as
limited in his potential by his education.

Another specialized career path for which preparatory education is
available relates to tax planning and compliance. It's possible to earn an
M.B.A. in taxation, and then become a tax manager within the financial
department of almost any corporation. This program is not generally
offered by traditional graduate schools of business.

Since at least one third of pretax corporate profit may have to be paid out in
taxes, the tax function is an important one, and it's entrusted to people with
special training. However, that doesn't by any means rule out the possibility
of rising from a tax job to a higher management position of broader scope.
Also, since taxation is not taught as a liberal art (!), it's generally possible to
enter an M.B.A. in tax program without any special preparation or work
experience.

*I wanted a professional skill with a degree as a credential. Most of
them—computer engineering, HR—require some kind of*

*undergraduate prerequisites in order to start graduate work. For
taxes, I only had to take two courses to get started.*

—Nancy, age 28

Other Advanced Degrees

A degree that certifies skills that are directly applicable to your job qualifies
you for higher pay and position. But an advanced degree that doesn't directly
relate to your job is unlikely to count in your favor. A college major in
English or classics will not work against you if you apply for business school,
law school, or a job. But a master's degree in such fields is unlikely to add to
your compensation. The opposite is true for degrees in technical subjects.

Computer systems is one of the fields in which the value of extra training is
recognized and rewarded. If you have a master's degree in this field, you will
very likely be able to start your work at a higher level and with greater
credibility. The extremely rapid growth of systems consulting firms testifies
to the widespread and urgent need for systems documentation, analysis,
enhancement, integration, and application. Here too, as is the case for
accounting and tax, a person who is seen as the repository of technical
expertise gains heavy leverage and authority. This advantage stays with you
even if you later move to a different function, or are promoted to a position
where you oversee other activities as well.

There are a number of other technical fields where master's degrees that are
available to well prepared students can add materially to their value and
employability. These range from engineering economics to construction
management, and extend into quite a number of scientific disciplines
needed in industry, such as solid state physics and cell biology. In a number
of these fields, people with doctorates are actively sought by employers.

After getting out of college I took over my father's construction company, and now it's a big one. We've found a small number of universities with excellent master's programs in construction, and that is where we prefer to hire our new management people.

—*Dexter, age 62*

Somehow or other, construction, along with the various other branches of engineering ranging from mechanical to nuclear, has managed to stick more than just its nose into the liberal arts temple. In terms of starting pay, graduating engineers earn more on average than graduates in traditional liberal arts fields. Many of these technical fields, however, have developed their depth of content to the point where at least a master's degree is needed if one is to be considered professionally qualified.

To enter a master's program, you will have needed to focus on its prerequisites and concentrate your undergraduate courses accordingly. Do not assume that merely completing a major makes you a good candidate to enter a master's program without major deficiencies, particularly if you want to switch to a different university. From the standpoint of immediate economic advantage, you will want to consider master's programs that can be completed in one year rather than two—there's considerable variation from one university to another.

A doctorate, at the other extreme, can take a virtually unlimited amount of time to complete, though one can try to finish the dissertation while holding a full-time job. Furthermore, even an uncompleted doctorate is apparently considered a valuable credential by some executives. For instance, publicity material on Christos Cotsakos, CEO of E-Trade Group, a leading Internet stock brokerage, makes a point of stating that he's currently writing his thesis to complete his doctorate at the University of London.

Similarly, publicity on Jerry Yang, a founder of Yahoo!, a still more prominent Internet firm, features the fact that he remains a candidate for a doctorate in electrical engineering at Stanford. Evidently the doctorate is the only degree so prestigious that even partial completion is thought to be something worth advertising. But other successful executives think differently.

> When I was young and foolish, I got a doctorate, but I almost never have mentioned it in my business career. People think Ph.D.'s are just technical people; they identify them with professors. Very theoretical and impractical. I don't need that.

—*CEO, Fortune 500 Company*

Law School

You will also see in management some people who got a degree in law rather than in business, as well as a much smaller number who got both a law and an M.B.A. degree. It's possible for lawyers to rise in management. Lawyers became CEOs of American Airlines and Monsanto Chemical, and another was president of the Card Division of American Express. In theory, a lawyer could be expected to have skills of analysis and exposition, to have the advantage of objectivity and perhaps of negotiating expertise. If the going got rough in management, he might also have the opportunity to retreat to a purely legal position.

Against these possible advantages we must count some negative factors. Law school takes three years, as opposed to two for an M.B.A. To get both degrees takes at least four years, and there's not much integration of the two programs. Of course, for some people the expanded timetable seems an attraction rather than a detriment.

My consulting firm wants almost everyone to go back for "more education" after two years of work, and I was happy to get a break. I chose law school. It seemed less competitive, the classes were smaller, and I had already been admitted. But it was a mistake. I'm bored to death, and I don't see how this is going to help me in consulting.

—Richard, age 25

However much or little you liked college—perhaps for reasons that didn't have much to do with the hours spent in the classroom—you are either going to like working more than you liked college, or quite possibly you are going to like it considerably less. If you don't like your job much, then the idea of going back to school, and for as long as possible, may seem quite compelling, particularly if it poses no financial problem.

But that is the wrong idea. Instead of seeking a temporary escape from your job that will last for as long as possible, it would make more sense to look for another kind of work that you will find more pleasing. Further education might serve to prepare you for that other kind of work. If not, going back to school may only cost you time and money.

After practicing law for a few years and not liking it, I managed to get a job as a junior consultant. The job had nothing to do with law. They said: "Your law degree doesn't get you higher pay here. If you shut up about it and you're lucky, maybe we'll forget you have it."

—Wyatt, age 33

Not everyone loves and respects lawyers. If you take a job that doesn't require a lawyer, your law degree is unlikely to add to your pay. But beyond that, career change is an awkward and potentially disturbing subject for an employer. A prospective employer is looking for stability and commitment, rather than a rebound.

What we have covered in this chapter are graduate degrees that may advance your career in business. Obviously, to become a doctor or a college professor, you also need an advanced degree. These are highly specific careers that generally have little overlap with the world of business, so we have not focused on them here. For comprehensive information on applying to advanced liberal arts or medical programs, see Kaplan's *Graduate School Admissions Adviser* and *Medical School Admissions Adviser*.

Who Do You Know?

Getting a job starts with getting an interview. It's easier to get an interview if you're already acquainted with someone in the company. The next best thing is to be recommended by a person who is known by someone in the company. At the very least, you need to know the name of the actual person who is doing the hiring. The person within the organization who knows you or to whom you have been recommended can help you not only in getting a first interview, but in the later phases of the hiring process.

> *If you don't see us on campus or don't know someone at the company, don't bother sending in your résumé to our corporate address. That won't do anything for you. You'll have to research our organization, get the name of one of our managers who actually does hiring, and write to him directly, individually.*
>
> —*Stephen Billard, Director of Software Development, Pacific Development Labs*

You have probably heard the somewhat flip observation that "What counts with these people is not *what* you know, but *who* you know." True, up to a point. What you know, such as facts you learn in courses and use to pass exams, has little to do with your usefulness to most employers. That's why most businesses don't give exams to decide who they will hire or promote.

In most jobs, it's your contribution to performance that matters. The ultimate hiring decision will therefore be based on what you are thought to be able to contribute to the organization's accomplishment. The issue is what you can do, not what you know. Being able to learn about unfamiliar situations and processes quickly and being able to find reliable sources of information and expertise count for more than knowing a lot of the answers on day one.

But you need to get an employer's attention first, so that you can show her what you're able to do.

> *Of the jobs I have held, there have been very few for which I actually had to formally apply. The contacts I made through volunteer and internship experiences during my college years helped me land a real job upon graduation.*
>
> —*Maritza Solari, Director of Medical Staff Services, California Pacific Medical Center*

The relevance of "who you know" and the importance of contacts in getting a first job is easy to understand if you put yourself on the other side of the desk to see how hiring works. Suppose you're looking to hire someone for a first job. In your file, you have some résumés. You also have some more complete job applications with supporting documents, and those would be even more time-consuming to read.

As you unenthusiastically ponder the question of how best to sort through this stack to choose someone to interview, the phone rings. It could be anyone you know—your cousin, your next door neighbor, a long-lost college buddy. With verve and conviction, this person starts telling you about a friend or acquaintance who will be graduating and wants a job. She gives you a summary of the person's résumé over the phone, and answers a couple of your questions.

Then, of course, she tells you, "You should interview him!" What are you going to say? "No, I am going to read 50 résumés before I decide on whom to interview," or, "Tell him to send his résumé to the personnel office?" No, more likely you will just agree, "Sure, thanks. I will do that. Have him call me for a date."

A recent survey of employers conducted by the University of Illinois Alumni Center highlights the importance of "employee referral" in recruiting. For college candidates, employers rated this method right behind on-campus recruiting activities. At the other extreme, "unsolicited applications" ranked number 11, next to last, for college candidates.

As an employer, once you agree to interview a candidate, you're committed to hearing and evaluating him. But that is a lot less unpleasant than plowing through a pile of unsolicited résumés. And if you're really lucky, you can interview this candidate quickly, check him out, hire him—and never even have to worry about how to sort through the other applicants. Because you have got too much to do, you will favor the solution that is near at hand.

When you contemplate hiring the recommended candidate, you will have one additional source of comfort, at least at the back of your mind: Someone has vouched for him. Maybe it's your neighbor, with whom you disagree on most things. Maybe it's your old college buddy, who knows absolutely nothing about your business. But at the very least, you can feel some confidence that this particular job seeker is not a total phony. You can also sense that if things don't work out, there will at any rate be someone with whom to split the blame, at least in your own mind.

Few people like to make an important decision alone. They prefer reinforcement or consensus. A colleague or a person you know who recommends someone for the job provides this consensus. The closer the recommender is to being a participant, the more likely he is to fulfill this need.

> *A person I'm going to hire usually interviews with several of my colleagues as well. But at the end of the day, the fact that that the candidate came to us recommended by someone counts also, if only because we need people to send us good candidates. We have to treat them right.*

—*Anson, age 33*

Who is Worth Knowing?

Lots of people are worth knowing because they are fun to be with, because you learn by being around them, or for plenty of other good reasons. But our subject here is what makes someone worth knowing because of the probability that he can help you get a good job.

The Guy in Charge

Bring this into focus from the top down. Who is the most worth knowing? Obviously, it's the person who will actually decide whom to hire for the job you most want. If you know him, your chances of getting the nod are tremendously improved, because most or all of the other candidates won't have this advantage.

> *The job I set my sights on was assistant to the executive chef of the best hotel here. He wasn't a difficult man to meet, and I learned that he had two assistants and hired one each year. I called or saw him a couple of times a year and began to kid him about putting my name down for 1996. I got the job!*

> *—Erica, age 23*

Erica's case is unusual. Most big shots or people in glamour jobs aren't so easy to meet. But what is more typical and hence more significant is the value of getting started early. The person you have known for a while will probably do more for you and express greater confidence in you than will the person you just met. The consistent desire and intention that you express over time is in itself a source of confidence. "She's had her heart set on this for a long time," your potential employer may think. "She's not going to mess up."

If Erica had decided in the end not to ask for or take that particular job, she would have lost nothing. With a little diplomacy, she would be able to retain the interest of a person who could probably refer her to others and help her in her career over a considerable period. The people you know whose work is relevant to your interests should likewise constitute an increasingly valuable resource, one that you can fall back on if things go wrong or that can propel and accelerate your progress when things go well.

Someone on the Inside

Most of the hiring for entry-level jobs is not done by highly visible, top level executives, however. It's done by supervisors or managers with limited seniority and visibility. As you focus on companies where you might like to work, you can think about ways of bringing yourself into contact with these people. Sometimes, it will turn out that you, your parents or a friend already knows someone who works where you want to work.

> *A friend of the family worked at Fidelity Investments. They had an internal temp department, and I went in and worked in six different positions, booking trades, answering phones, typing invoices. I got a lot of interviews just because I had Fidelity Investments on my résumé. Having a brand name on your résumé is extremely helpful. Also, I don't think I would have gotten the job without the help of the family friend. The network of people you know will have an effect on your career.*
>
> *—Sharon Spooler, age 25*

If you don't have a contact at a target company, don't despair. There are ways you can develop contacts at a company yourself. For example, at least a year before you plan to do your serious job hunting, pick up a recruiting brochure of a company you're interested in, and call. Ask for an informational interview or the opportunity to observe someone on the job. Don't pressure the person you meet for a job offer. The idea is to demonstrate interest in the company and make a friendly business contact.

> *Every company puts a contact name on their data forms in the career planning office. It's no mystery—just call the person up! I will get students who call me up and say that they are very excited*

about the company and want the name of a sales rep in their area so they can travel with him for a day. That shows genuine interest in the company.

—Jim Gwinn, Director of Global Staffing, American Cyanamid Company

If you invest your effort, for instance in spending a day with a salesman, you will learn. And you will get more than that back. Establishing a friendly acquaintance with someone inside the company gets your foot in the door. If and when an appropriate job for you becomes available, your contact can often give you advance notice and put in a good word for you with whomever is doing the hiring.

Calling a local office is a more direct way of making contact.

I felt that IBM was going to make a comeback, and in my freshman year I called the local sales office and asked to speak to the manager. I told him I loved IBM and wanted to come in and get some advice. Over the next two years, I was invited to sales conferences and spent time with salesmen. That office didn't have internships, but they made me a great job offer.

—John, age 26

How many calls do you think that manager gets from college students wanting to come in and talk about selling for IBM? Outside the recruiting season, he's likely to get scarcely any at all. After all, he's not advertising for job candidates. You need some initiative even to find him.

Such a call is flattering for the manager. It offers an agreeable way of spending "working" time. Even from the standpoint of public relations, a manager of a major corporation is unlikely to refuse when asked to speak with a student. Furthermore, if he's not interested in you as a prospective employee, he will probably be willing to tell you why. This information can be helpful as you adjust your priorities and directions of effort.

> Most freshmen and sophomores don't feel confident even about the type of job or employer they want, and they certainly don't feel ready to express strong affinity for any particular company. Do what you need to do to get an internship or job where you can find out more.

If you learn about companies, you will find good things, appealing things about some of them. If you're curious or ambitious, you will then want to learn more.

> *I recommend doing internships in a bunch of different industries. I interned at Merrill Lynch, in the accounting department of a natural gas company and at a chemical company. These experiences helped me to figure out what I ultimately wanted to do.*
>
> —*Ryan Mossman, age 25*

Check your phone book. Call the home or regional office of a company in an industry you find interesting and ask for local plant or sales office phone numbers. You won't be wasting anyone's time, because no one is uninterested in snaring good talent. You will also learn what kinds of things people like to say about their jobs, and what kind of reactions and questions they expect from you, all of which will come in very handy later. In effect, you will be able to take a trial run at communicating with prospective employers, without having to face the high stakes of senior year interviewing. The more you interview, the better you will get at it.

Within an industry, or within a functional field such as finance or marketing, each person that you know can bring you into contact with others. This expands your knowledge of the field and widens your set of business acquaintances, putting you in a position to hear about and take advantage of good job opportunities. That is what John did after establishing contact with IBM.

> *I asked my friend at IBM to tell me about some of the younger and smaller computer industry companies near us. Then I asked him whether he knew some interesting people at the companies which sounded the most appropriate to me. This actually led to the job offer I accepted.*
>
> *—John, age 26*

You might wonder why any of these people would be interested in talking to John, or to you. The answer is that they probably need you more than you need them. You need only one employer. A business, however, will maintain its vitality only if it's effective in finding enough enthusiastic and interested new people, not only to replace those who will inevitably leave, but also to expand. There's also a natural desire to help anyone who is exercising initiative and trying to get ahead.

Someone Who Knows Someone

As John's example indicates, the people you know can help you by getting other people interested in you, or by telling you whom to call next.

Unfortunately, it's often difficult to assess whether a person is going to have a large circle of relevant acquaintances into which he will gladly draw you, or whether he's a loner, or simply reluctant to bring the people he knows into touch with each other.

> *Don't feel uncomfortable about using every connection you have. Ask the people you know to meet with you to tell you about what they do. People are generally happy to speak with you if you're not asking for a job up front. After you meet with them, send a follow-up thank you letter and a copy of your résumé. Get your résumé in the system and you will have an initial connection with the company that you can build on.*
>
> —*Aaron Katz, age 25*

It's best to make multiple efforts, without feeling that each one is a tough test of your talent and will. Learn as you go along. This is a lot different from taking courses. In starting to develop each contact, you're not committed to making a great effort, and you don't risk a big loss if one of your choices doesn't pan out.

> *I took a course in industrial sociology and my term project involved documenting examples of differing management cultures. I made blind calls to people at quite a few companies. Most were at least willing to talk. About a quarter of them are now in my card file. Those are people I wouldn't worry about asking for help.*
>
> —*Rita, age 24*

Some of the people Rita called might have given her a "C" for competence or personality—if they had had the chance. But unlike instructors or TAs, they didn't have the chance and they never will. In making contacts, only your successes count. You can and should be much bolder in deciding how to apply your effort than you can afford to be at school. Rita did well in her course, but the new contacts she made had more value to her than the high grade. With some insight and initiative, you can make many nonbusiness courses count towards your future.

In most cases, your contact at a company will not actually be the person who ultimately hires you. To what degree a contact is ultimately effective in getting you treated differently from those who merely mailed in résumés depends on the nature and particularly the closeness of the relationship between the person who recommends you and the person you hope will act on that recommendation. Mere position or reputation is not enough.

> *I love politics, and I'd been active on behalf of our mayor, who's very popular. He was happy to write a bunch of people for me. Unfortunately, this turned out to be helpful only if they had had personal dealings with him, or at least wanted to. Otherwise, I guess they just thought he was paying off a political debt.*

—Aaron, age 23

This illustrates a more general observation. In job hunting, letters of recommendation do very little good unless there's already some kind of relationship or at least a personal acquaintance between the recommender and the recipient of the letter.

If a person is willing to help you, he can help you more by putting you in contact with people who know him than he can by writing letters to the people you want to convince to hire you.

It's also better to get two or three contacts that are personal and incisive, rather than a sheaf of relatively mechanical and standard letters. Giving yourself time and proceeding across strong and short links rather than shooting for the moon, you're far more likely to hit your target.

> *My uncle really wanted to help. He wrote a bunch of letters, and he made some phone calls while I was right there in his office. It was those phone calls that got the results: "Let's make a date for Tom to see you right now, while you're on the line."*
>
> *—Tom, age 25*

You may not have an uncle who can help you, but you will have other contacts and you can influence how they go about trying to help you. Don't be afraid to ask for what you need—whether it's a name and number for you to call or an interview time and date—as specifically as possible. You shouldn't assume that people know how they can be most effective in helping you, and you should be sure that you're clear and precise in your requests for help and recommendations.

Your Classmates

Most of the people you meet during your college years will be students. This large group can give you tremendous aid and support later on.

> *My college friends have been helpful to me throughout my career. Talking with them about what they do and what they find enjoyable about their jobs has provided me with an additional perspective on my own career.*
>
> *—Steve Bowsher, E*Trade Group*

A great many of your college friends will be classmates. Although classmates can be helpful once everyone is working, their personal contribution to possibilities for your first job will typically be very limited. This is primarily because they just don't know very many people who are already working. The longer you work, the more people with hiring potential you know. But there's more to it than that. If you take an interest in people, and if you have a pleasant, flattering, unintrusive curiosity about their lives, then you will find many doors open for you.

> *Many people like to chat about their families and their work. One girl's mother turned out to work for an affiliate of the company I was most interested in. Actually, both of them were flattered when I asked if I could meet the mother. I got the hiring interview with no trouble, and everyone was delighted.*

> *—Jamie, age 24*

If you make a list of a dozen student friends with whom you feel comfortable talking, you will most likely find two things that surprise you. First, you will be surprised by how little you really know about the work or the employment relationships of their parents and others who are important in their lives. Second, you will probably find at least one potential contact that you so far have not bothered to act on, or even think about. This is an exercise worth trying.

We tend to categorize people and relationships. There are the people you like to be with. Then there are the other people with whom you share interests or activities. Still another group are relatives, friends of friends, and others with whom you're drawn into associating, without ever really deciding to do so. And finally, maybe, there are a few people who you're thinking of specifically as job hunting resources. Everyone is neatly pushed into their pigeon holes. Problem is, this is a recipe for lost opportunity because virtually every person in any of these categories has the potential to contribute to your job search. Talk work with your classmates about their job aspirations. It's a subject of near universal interest. These conversations will lead to information and opportunities.

In these kinds of relationships, it's important to give as good as you get. If you can help your friends by putting them in touch with one of your parents or business contacts, do so. Even if they can't return the favor right now, they will probably be able—and will definitely be willing—to offer you assistance in the future.

Upperclassmen

Students in the classes above yours have even greater potential to help you. Some will probably be hired by firms you're interested in. If you are heedless and oblivious, you won't even know when this happens. Don't expect your alumni association or placement office to automatically send you employment information on recent graduates. Most of them don't work that way. They are happy just to keep up with the home addresses.

> *After I was far into the interviewing process with my number 1 target company, I discovered working there a girl two years ahead of me with whom I had been friendly. She helped me. But I felt stupid not even knowing she was there—she would have been glad to help from the beginning.*
>
> *—Theresa, age 23*

Pay attention to the graduating seniors—every single year. Find out what they will be doing, and where. Plan to stay in touch if there is reason to do so. These days, the Internet makes this quick and painless. You may not get every new phone number, but you can always re-establish contact through your friends' parents or on the Internet.

Classmates and older students whom you know can also give you invaluable information about the hiring process. They can tell you what they learned in interviews, and how the interviews are conducted. Their successes and failures can help you figure out the hiring criteria and standards applied by different employers. This information can make your own job campaign more realistic and effective. You can benefit from the same kind of input even during the months that you're involved in interviewing.

> I would run across the same people at the placement office, signing up, waiting for interviews. We started to organize informal sessions at the end of the day, where we would exchange observations and ideas about the interviews. I learned much faster this way.

—*Thomas, age 22*

Fellow Members of Clubs, Societies, and Teams

Getting hired is a common interest that almost everyone shares, and is willing to talk about. Other common interests can also bring you together with students who can help you get hired.

One reason to engage in activities ranging from team sports to debating to the engineering society is to meet people, namely, fellow students. But activities differ starkly in their business contact potential, and some, though not all, of the differences are evident from the beginning. For instance, as a dorm rep or in a large fraternity or sorority, you will have ready access to quite a large number of students. Indeed, almost every hour of effort you put into these activities can broaden and deepen these contacts.

> *I had two main activities in college: crew and student council. Crew had lots of prestige, and student council had none. But council gave me an excuse to be everywhere and meet everyone. Crew turned out to be rather solitary, though I made a couple of close friends.*

> —*Alex, age 23*

Exposure to opportunity is valuable only to the extent that you're prepared and motivated to exploit that opportunity. Many student council members, social chairmen, and other students who have access to or actually cultivate a wide circle of acquaintances nevertheless do very little to make this "people power" effective in generating job possibilities and offers. The problem is partly one of attitude.

Many people feel uncomfortable talking about jobs or asking for help. You shouldn't. In talking jobs with your friends, you're not exploiting them. You're pursuing a mutual advantage.

Alternatively, if you join a small and closely knit organization, or one that is oriented primarily to outreach beyond the college, then whatever else you may accomplish or get out of this experience, you probably won't be getting a proportionate return on effort in the form of contacts. Small teams and many social service activities tend to turn out this way. You can't always tell in advance, but you should be at least as flexible about your extra-curriculars as you are about your program of study.

Obviously, there's more to life than job hunting, and you should certainly participate in clubs or teams you find fulfilling or fun. But seriously consider making time for some activities that will give you the chance to meet people who can help you in your career.

Professors

Professors who have access to the world of employers because they consult or have worked outside the college can be valuable sources of contacts.

> *I took a course in urban studies with a part-time professor and got an A in the course. That professor then hired me as an urban planning intern. At the time, I didn't think of cultivating the professor to get a job—the opportunity arose and I took it. In hindsight, though, I would definitely recommend developing mentoring relationships with professors.*
>
> —*Eliot Cohen, Media Relations Manager, Phillip Morris Asia*

This wasn't a long shot. A part-time professor almost surely works in his field outside the college, and hence will have useful contacts. (Some visiting professors are regularly employed in industry or government also.) In a field such as urban studies, it's logical to expect teachers to have real-world connections. The same is true in computer sciences.

> *Professors often consult with industrial organizations, and this relationship can provide an entree for students. They may be able to work on one-time projects, find a summer job or even a full-time job upon graduation.*
>
> —*Roy Levin, Director, Systems Research Center, Digital Equipment Corporation*

In certain subjects, such as economics or statistics, some professors are entirely academic in their interests, while others are very active in consulting and other nonacademic pursuits. It's up to you to find out who is in a position to help. Often professors have résumés or lists of publications available, either online or through their departments, that at least give a broad hint about their interests and activities. You can also ask them where they have worked or consulted.

> *I developed a strong mentoring relationship with the chairman of the economics department. He introduced me to consulting, which I ultimately chose to do.*
>
> —*Mary Falvey, self-employed consultant*

In other departments, such as history or English, professors are less likely to have their toes in the mainstream flowing towards employment, though many can help if your interest is in writing. A professor as mentor can be very helpful in making your college more experience more successful and thus indirectly enhancing your job prospects, even if she is not in a position to put you in touch with an organization that will hire you.

Alumni

Alumni are an important resource for most colleges, and they can be for students also. Alumni often rank right behind reputation and placement office services among the top job-getting advantages that your college can contribute.

The alumni network is extremely undervalued. If anyone at Princeton called me, I would do just about anything to help him or her.

—Sharon Spooler, age 25

"I would do just about anything to help him or her." Those are strong words. And there's no reason to think that they are only applicable or particularly applicable to Princeton alumni.

In small colleges, your relationships with members of your own class are likely to be much tighter than the relationships between students from large universities. But don't assume that alumni of a large university are indifferent to the old school and its students, merely because of the large numbers of people involved. It's more likely to work the other way around, as the alumni reach a critical mass in the community. Alumni of many state universities, for example, constitute formidable, highly committed, and even dominant groups in many sectors of business life.

Professors and administrators can often connect you with alumni who can be of help.

Use your connections. My college dean and master were invaluable to me in my job search. They put me in touch with alumni working in the field I was interested in.

—Elizabeth, age 22

In the best case, the benefits can be spectacular:

When I was a sophomore, our football team was losing almost every week. Then Billy came in as quarterback, and we lost only half our games. It was still a losing year, but to the alumni Billy was a big winner. He was taken care of for his first job, and everything after that.

—*Tod, 35*

No matter where you went to college, almost any alumnus will be more willing to talk with you than with someone who doesn't share this experience with her. Furthermore, many alumni stay closely involved with teams or activities that were important to them as students.

We can't all be football stars, but in any college there are a number of student activities that engender strong alumni support. Both the number of alumni involved and the intensity of their enthusiasm are important.

For our school newspaper, we have one alumni advisor, and there's one meeting a year that around ten alumni attend. But we have a little booklet with lots of alumni addresses and phone numbers. The ones in journalism will really go out of their way to help any of us.

—*Sally, age 24*

That is an important distinction. In many schools, football alumni are not only numerous, they populate almost every sector of business, finance, and even government. However, alumni who feel affinity with a specialized student activity, such as the newspaper or the debate team, are likely to be concentrated in the corresponding career paths. Not every college newspaper hound goes into journalism as a career, but those who do are likely to take a far stronger interest in their successors at the college paper than are those who don't. To get leverage from an alumni group, you need to share not just a student activity but a work interest with them. Otherwise, though they will surely desire to help you, most of them won't be able to do much for you.

Just the existence of an updated list of the alumni of a student organization is a strong indicator of interest, and the potential for help. The football team has lists of supporters, season ticket holders, and the like. If you're wondering whether participation in the lacrosse team or in the Student Democratic Club is going to give access to alumni help, just find out whether there is an up-to-date list of interested alumni. If there is, then assess its length and its quality. For your purpose, the quality of the list depends on where and in what capacity these people work. You should also ask about any events that bring current students into contact with alumni. You're not likely to choose your college activities entirely on the basis of their value in facilitating contact with useful alumni. But you shouldn't ignore the possibility.

Student activities are by no means the only way of getting to know alumni who can help you. To an increasing extent, alumni directories are becoming available in digital form, for instance as CDs. You will be able to search this data by name of employer, by location, or by key words such as sales or electronics. People put their names in such directories because they want to be in contact with alumni and students. You shouldn't hesitate to call them. On average, they will be less motivated to help than those with whom you share an activity that was important to both of you, but they are not likely to hang up on you either.

I was interested in working in the best bank in Ohio. On a whim, I flipped through the alumni book. It wasn't too hard to find several alumni working there, just by checking the geographical index.

When I called, some of them had already moved on. But almost all the ones I found were able and willing to help.

—Alison, age 22

The most interested alumni tend to be those who have updated their listings. Even if only 20 percent of the graduates from recent classes are listed, these will be the 20 percent who are most enthusiastic and eager. Many classes publish their own lists or booklets, for instance at their fifth and tenth reunions and at intervals thereafter. These publications often contain more detailed information about class members' activities and interests. The alumni office may not have these books, but you can get at them via individual members of the classes.

Your college alumni magazine can also be a valuable resource. Most of these magazines have alumni "reporters" who put together the notes for each class, and in the notes you will also get information on who's working where. Even without contacting the reporter, you can probably find an alumnus through the main number at her place of work.

An alumnus who took a job at one of your target companies, particularly a recent alumnus, can be an especially valuable find. He will have first hand knowledge of how that company recruits at your campus. He can also tell you a lot about what they are looking for in selecting students.

Other Contacts

People whom you know or can approach are by no means limited to those you meet through college affiliations. It's entirely wrong to imagine that when you express interest in a company, or in employment, you're asking them to do you a favor. The exact opposite is often the case.

I am somewhat prominent in my ethnic community. Frankly, a big insurance company pays me an annual retainer for my help in recruiting. They only need to hire a few agents a year from among us, but they are very happy with what I bring in.

—*Morris, age 62*

You can help Morris earn his pay by showing some genuine interest in a job. Even those who are not paid specifically to recruit know that recruiting generates value for their employer and hence for them. For example, if you're interested in computer science, you will naturally go to computer shows, where many manufacturers are represented. Most of the company representatives at the show will be marketers of some kind, but some will also have other backgrounds.

> Everyone who works for a company is a potential recruiter for that company.

I was interested in robotics and went to an ISEE conference, where a number of companies had booths that seemed to be aimed primarily in generating interest in their products. There was almost no recruiting literature, but it turned out they all wanted good engineers!

—*Robin, age 29*

Many trade shows and consumer product shows have panels or open-house meetings specifically devoted to recruiting. At such meetings, you can be sure that all the companies represented are looking to hire. However, you may be surrounded by students seeking the same jobs you are. Be prepared for an off-the-cuff mini-interview, and carry extra copies of your résumé.

Do Extracurriculars Make a Difference?

9

The previous chapters of this book explored the ways in which your college studies and your performance in them can affect your job possibilities. You will see in the next chapter what interviewees had to say about the role of term-time and summer work and internships in qualifying students for jobs. The subject of this chapter is everything else that you do during your college years. This includes sports, other extracurriculars, social organizations, and noncollege activities. One way in which all these activities can affect your job possibilities is through the contacts they provide, a subject that was the focus of the previous chapter. We will look now at other ways in which these activities can add to your employability and effectiveness.

Remember, this is not a book about being happy, popular, or successful in college. This book is about how you can use your college experiences to prepare yourself for a great job. We are talking about one limited dimension of life. No doubt, you have concerns, needs, and desires that don't involve jobs at all. All of us do. A lot of what you choose to do in college will reflect these other interests or needs. However, to the degree that a satisfying job is important to you, you may have to make compromises between your job goals and your other priorities.

It may seem harsh to have to ask yourself very frequently, "How much would this do for my résumé?" Or, "What could I do with this job that would impress an interviewer?" It's up to you to strike a continuing balance between what you want to do, what you know is worthwhile and will give you satisfaction, and what is most likely to yield dividends when you go job hunting and afterwards. In the best case, these may coincide. The same will be true after you start working, when you need to consider future choices of jobs and assignments at least partially in terms of their impact on your qualifications and résumé.

What Do Your Activities Say About You?

My experiences as dorm president and doing sports and campus theater provided me with time management, and organizational and teamwork skills that have been essential to me in my career.

—Mark May, Senior Consultant, IBM

Surely those experiences were enjoyable and fulfilling, but what is relevant here is that they bore fruit later in relation to employment. But how, if at all, did these activities help Mark get a job with IBM? What conclusions might an employer draw about a person who participated in sports and theater? What conclusions might an employer come to about you, based on your choice of activities?

Every job and every employer is somewhat different, but there are a few general requirements common to all or most hiring situations. The broadest requirement is that as an employer you want someone who succeeds, who gets things done. That is one reason GPA is important. A high GPA highlights a student as a winner, even if her academic tasks were very largely irrelevant to what she will need to do at work. But you can get a high GPA without having had to cooperate with or lead other people. And those are activities that are highly important in a great many jobs.

We look for a background of achievement, a strong indication of leadership and the ability to juggle and stand up under pressure.

—Senior banker, major investment firm

You will get very similar descriptions of the ideal candidate from a wide variety of companies. Almost all employers want people who are cooperative, yet able to lead. They want people who can handle pressure, but know how to budget their time so that their work doesn't suffer. They often want creative thinkers who like new challenges and can take initiative in tackling those challenges. Many of these qualities are best demonstrated outside of class, through extracurricular activities.

Leadership Positions

The importance of teamwork and leadership in business and other organizations explains the fact that many employers are impressed by any applicant whose college years included conspicuous interpersonal successes, such as becoming captain of a major team. After all, to be elected captain, you have to develop skills that go beyond the techniques of the game. You have to collaborate with and lead others. If you have been chosen as captain, it means that your fellow teammates felt your leadership could make a special contribution to helping them win.

Now, which is more relevant to being a successful director of research or a hotel manager: getting an A in microeconomics or making a big contribution to winning college hockey games as captain of the team? You might think it obvious that success in microeconomics is more relevant. In fact, it's pretty much a toss-up. Neither microeconomic production functions nor effectiveness in executing body checks have much direct connection with creating value in an organization, but both of these successes at least demonstrate your capacity for developing and applying relevant skills and for consistent, well-directed effort. Each achievement is a plus, but neither constitutes convincing proof that you will succeed at work.

Not every interviewer is going to be turned on by each of your college achievements. This is a fact that you will need to greet with understanding rather than with shock:

> I was pretty big on our campus, and a few interviewers identified with that and admired it. But others were more mousy guys who almost seemed to resent my prominence. Practically every one of these people stressed that "work is different from college."

—Kirby, age 22

Sounds like Kirby didn't track well with some of his interviewers, and he probably lost some opportunities as a result. Going from your senior year of college to a job is like going from a big-time high school senior to a low-status college freshman. You just have to stop thinking of yourself as a big deal.

One way in which work is different from college is that you rise to the top of your campus in just two or three years. At work, it generally takes far longer to get anywhere near the top. But the person who makes the final decision to hire you for an entry-level position is going to be much more interested in your chances of being an initial success at the job than in your potential ultimately to become a top executive. After all, he's unlikely to be rewarded or punished for where you end up 20 years from now, and in any case no one can see that far ahead with any clarity.

The key question hanging over the hiring process will be your likely effectiveness in your first assignments. This effectiveness will depend in part on your ability to work well with others. If you're the captain, or a starting player, then you have risen to the top level of skill and effectiveness in your chosen activity. You have been able to cooperate with and win acceptance from others in a collaborative situation. If you were excessively selfish or closed in on yourself as a person, then you probably would not have made the grade.

> *Working in an organization, you learn to respect the people above you. It's a must. So, whatever I thought when I was in college myself, I think I have more respect for a college senior I interview if he held a leadership position while in college.*
>
> *—Frank, age 28*

Your accomplishment in becoming head of a fraternity or other organization will probably be seen in a similar light. Whether you actually achieved anything in the job is probably beyond the power of the interviewer or employer to evaluate. He will most likely take your word for it, as expressed in your résumé or interviews. It's your success in advancing to the top position that is most likely to be viewed as an objective and significant fact.

> If you have been appreciated and moved ahead in one group based on the quality of your work with others, this implies that you will probably be successful in another organization, such as your employer's.

Potential employers look for you to be a team player and a leader. My experiences as dorm counselor, cheerleader, sorority member and coordinator of the freshman orientation program provided ample evidence of my ability in these areas.

—*Lara, age 26*

If you have held a conspicuous leadership position, you can expect to have to talk about what challenges you faced, what decisions you made, and what results you achieved. It will be not only nice, but necessary that you have available concise, compelling, plausible, and, above all, interesting answers to these natural questions.

I was president of a small sorority. The interviewers had never heard of the sorority, but I could sense they were curious about how I got to be president, and what I did there.

—*Janet, age 22*

Put yourself in the position of an interviewer, one who is not well acquainted with sororities, or at least not in any positive way. What does he think goes on? Better organization of all-weekend drinking parties? A ten-year file of term papers? Struggles with an archaic national organization that opposes minority membership? Better to focus on something concrete and positive.

What could Janet do at the sorority, and what could she say about her experience there that would make her more attractive to employers? Perhaps she could mobilize alumnae, in person and via the Internet, to share information about jobs and about career education. This system of networking might be extended from her local chapter to the region and then the whole country.

Or perhaps Janet could resolve current financial problems at the sorority and put her organization on a sound financial footing for the future. Perhaps she could bring the membership policies up to date, to attract people who are achievers. Most likely there are plenty of possibilities, because what most students want now is not what most of them wanted in 1950, and every organization tends to follow its rut rather than to renew itself for the future.

In business, what counts is whether you win or lose, and by what score. It's ironic that in this particular respect, athletic and other teams have a focus that is most congruent with that of business.

> *Every potential employer will want you to be able to prove that you know how to be a team player and can take on different roles within the team structure. The fact that I had been a varsity basketball player for four years showed that I worked well in a team.*
>
> *—Steve Bowsher, E*Trade Group*

The French club or the social committee don't particularly win or lose, but a basketball team certainly does. If you lose, you better have something more to tell than just a list of mistakes that you are sure you won't make the next time out.

Our team lost nine out of fourteen games. Local interviewers asked about that, but after a few tries I developed quite an effective pitch, beginning with how practically all the starters graduated last year. I got credit for courage under adversity and for scoring a great turn-around.

—Norman, age 23

Being captain, or a major player, makes you an expert. Getting that far gives you an aura of success, even if the team didn't do well. So, explanations and excuses fall on receptive ears. If the team improved so much under your leadership that it lost much less badly than before, then you're okay. It's like taking a company that is losing $10 million per year, and going through a first round of improvements that reduces the losses to $1 million per year. That is not an ideal and perfect performance, but it's a valuable one.

Overall, the logic may be imperfect, but it's difficult to negate: If you have been recognized as effective in one organization, then you're likely to be effective in another.

Of course, it matters which organization has been the site of your successes. If it's thought to be large and to harbor highly ambitious and competitive people, so much the better. If it's small and low-key, then your success in it is likely to be discounted accordingly. But an interviewer or hiring manager generally can't be expected to know anything about all the organizations on your campus. He will likely accept your explanations about the size and achievements of your own organization. In fact, your position as head of the society or organization is likely to lend credence to your explanation of its accomplishments.

I was only the membership chairman of our campus political organization, but I could talk pretty well about how I had led the campaign which doubled our membership. That counts as successful sales experience, and I think it counted very heavily.

—Diane, age 24

As a leader or officer of a significant team, sorority, or organization, you will get some credit for working with others and getting results—especially if you're able to give a compelling account of how these results were obtained. Recruiters won't know exactly where you ranked in your organization's hierarchy. They won't know just who did what to whom. If you can find your own horn and blow it, then you can find your interviewer's hot button.

Nonleadership Roles in Clubs and Other Groups

Mere membership in one or any number of student groups, even if they are very successful groups, is unlikely to gain you the same credit as a leadership role. Membership may show that you're a "joiner," or even that you're personable and personally acceptable. But it won't show much about your capacity to get a job done.

Your involvement with student activities does say something about your willingness to get out, meet, and be with other people. Your ability to function as an active member of a social or recreational group suggests that you will be comfortable and compatible with social relationships in the work organization. However, in many companies this factor is of distinctly less importance than it would have been in the past. Social considerations count for much less in filling the vast majority of jobs than they did 50 years ago. The management pool is much more of a melting pot now than it was in 1950, harboring people of vastly different backgrounds, interests and orientations. These people are not required to have common interests or to see and enjoy each other outside the office.

> *Back when I was hired, Personnel felt a responsibility for seeing to it that each new person would "fit in." If someone was "different," that was a potential problem. Today, the world has turned upside down. Diversity rather than uniformity is the goal.*

—*Harry, age 57*

So a fondness for parties and other social gatherings and a tendency to want to spend lots of time with others won't necessarily be seen as a plus unless your chosen career necessarily involves heavy socializing with clients. Your memberships are not likely to do much to enhance your attractiveness unless the organizations to which you belonged are extremely selective in some relevant way, or unless you have won what you can convincingly describe as conspicuous leadership roles in them.

> *Anyone who's been to college knows that you can sign up for as many organizations as you want, and count yourself as a member of them. Numbers don't count. When I read CVs and interview seniors, what I want to see is quality of accomplishment.*

—*Sam, age 28*

It's not the amount of time you put in or the number of organizations you join that assures a positive result. When it comes to the job market, you may get out either a lot more or a lot less than you had put into your activities. Think ahead abut what you're going to have to show for your participation. And think particularly about how it's going to show, how you're going to be able to make it visible.

Starting Up a New Organization

One way to stand out is by starting, or reviving, an organization. This may require more initiative, but there's distinctly less competition, and less uncertainty about the results. Instead of working hard and waiting several years to see where you get, as a founder you can win rather rapid and reliable return on your effort. You're not dependent on getting elected, and you don't have to spend time doing the scut work until promoted to something better.

Most colleges make it easy to register a new organization and impose only minimal requirements. If you're even a little bit outgoing, it can be easy to sign up members, because little or no commitment is required of them. Making the new group actually come to life and act will be harder.

It adds an extra plus if your organization has a theme that relates in a timely way to your career goals. Forming a financial management society might sound a little stiff, but how about a World Investment Club? Being able to say that you signed up 100 members would sound great. Being able to talk about worthwhile activities you carried out will also help.

Our college gives no encouragement at all for anything related to business; they hate business. So, with my roommate, I did the obvious: we created a Future Managers Club. We acquired a few basic books, invited speakers and set up trips, liaised with the Placement Office—and we got a lot of members. It's the most satisfying and useful project I ever undertook, and it's constantly getting bigger and better.

—Karen, age 22

Think about what would have helped you, what you would like to have had, in relation to your own future, and most likely you will find many classmates who think as you do. Every company wants self starters. They want spark plugs. They want people who can see and meet a need without having to wait for specific permission and direction. If you show initiative you will be sought after, because initiative is rare and very valuable.

At Procter & Gamble, we value curiosity, enthusiasm, and innovation. We want people who are never satisfied with the status quo and constantly strive to do better.

—John Pepper, CEO, Procter & Gamble

This is a theme that CEOs, executives, and other managers touch on almost every time they talk about whom they want to hire. What would you do with someone who was good only at following instructions and at doing the same thing over and over again? Would you put him in the advertising or product development department? Or would you hire him, if at all, only to hold down a place on the assembly line, or to fill out routine forms?

The most valuable person to hire is the one who can solve new problems rather than merely apply old solutions, and who can create something new out of nothing when needed. Creating a new organization shows that you are this kind of person. But every experience that stretches your capacity and understanding will improve your ability to show that you are indeed a self-starter. This is one more filter to apply in screening the activities in which you might want to participate.

Seek out groups and situations that will enable you to find new solutions and better ways to do things. In a tough and demanding setting, any outcome at all can be interpreted as having some positive value.

> The year before I came, a student enterprise that provided moving, rental, and other services had gone broke. What a mess! Who'd want to take it on? I did, because no one else wanted to. Besides, anything I did would be an improvement. That's how it worked out—very well indeed.
>
> —Barney, age 25

You don't have to play the hero. All you have to do is avoid joining the lemmings that rush to meet the same big wave. Instead of that, find a hole in the dike to plug. Disasters are uncommon, but any nonathletic student activity you can choose is probably going to be greatly improvable and expandable. At most colleges, a great many people spend endless hours competing to become reporters for the school newspaper. Currently, not very many direct their attention to new publications and alternative media, such as the Internet. You could get to be editor of your paper's Internet edition without facing a great deal of competition.

If you enjoy competing (even when the odds are against you and the required effort is large), fine. But recognize why you're doing it. Don't assume that your chance of becoming editor-in-chief (generally an unlikely possibility) will justify your choosing to indulge your penchant for this kind of scrambling and writing, rather than choosing an activity that has a greater probability of facilitating your job-getting effort.

Community Service Activities

When you were in high school, you were probably advised that it would be useful to have some community service on your record. Colleges want students who are interested and giving members of their communities. Whether by natural inclination or with ulterior motives, you can put in some time at hospitals or soup kitchens.

What does this kind of giving have to do with your getting hired by a profit-making business? Not very much in itself. Most businesses would rather hire giving people than selfish people, but there are many qualities that they seek and have difficulty in finding that rank higher on the priority list than unselfishness. Think about what an employer would glean from the following recital:

> *I volunteered for two years for the public defender's office, interviewing prisoners and organizing help for them. I was able to change our process so that the same number of volunteers could accomplish more for three times as many detainees.*
>
> —*Elizabeth, age 23*

Now, if you were an employment interviewer, what would you get out of this? It suggests that Elizabeth has a desire to help the unfortunate. You may or may not share that desire—perhaps a 50-50 shot, certainly not a clear win for Elizabeth. As a hiring manager, maybe you think more petty criminals should be in jail, rather than let out because of the efforts of people such as Elizabeth.

Reading along a different axis, it looks like Elizabeth has taken an inefficient system and, working from the bottom, has managed to change it dramatically to make it much more effective. That is plausible, because a great many business people suspect that all government and nonprofit systems are hopelessly inefficient. In this context, Elizabeth looks like an agent of change, and the change has worked out admirably.

> Few people can claim to have made important changes in their organizations. Can you? If so, you have an interviewing ace in the hole. If you can't make this claim now, think about ways you might improve the function of any group you work with or belong to. Follow through on your ideas. Changing things for the better shows exactly the kind of initiative employers are looking for.

Community service activities can be worthwhile and fulfilling. They can also be good for your job prospects if you look for ways to be both an active and proactive participant. Don't just volunteer at the homeless shelter— seek new sources of funding or new corporate sponsorship for the shelter. Don't just work as an adult literacy instructor—organize a recruiting campaign to enlist more volunteers. Initiative and leadership in the name of a good cause will be admired by potential employers.

Your Interests and Pastimes

Hiring managers view your nonwork interests from differing angles. Some employers are rigorous:

> *Someone's résumé is not likely to show up on my desk unless he or she has the grades and requisite qualifications. From there, I look hard for discriminators such as hobbies and outside interests. I look to see whether the candidate's hobbies involve discipline. There's a big difference between a candidate who says he's interested in music and a candidate who is a concert pianist.*

> —Dr. Martin Brotman, president and CEO, California Pacific Medical Center

Other employers focus on how important your nonwork interests are in your life. Sit down again in the hirer's chair. Suppose you have two candidates who are otherwise equally qualified. One spends a lot of time on personal interests, hobbies, individual sports, and family activities. The other seems already to be married to his work. He's deeply into his field of study and projected career, and he spends only the minimum time on anything else. This exaggerates the contrast, cartooning it to make the distinction easier to evaluate. But which candidate is more appealing?

There's no simple right way to resolve this choice. Here are two diametrically opposite readings:

> *When I hire, I want to see a complete person. Not someone who will obsess, burn out, or throw a bomb at every obstacle. If there's nothing in your life but work, I won't like you.*

> —Ronald, corporate recruiter, age 26

"The people who succeed here work very hard at it. Yes, they stay late, and they come in weekends, and they get tired. The person who has done fine up to now without stretching isn't the person I want. Because he's going to get stretched here, and I don't know how he'll stand up to that.

—Miriam, recruitment coordinator, age 31

Problem is, if you were interviewed by both Ronald and Miriam, it might not be obvious which of them was looking for workaholics and which of them hated workaholics. They don't wear signs telling you what they're looking for, and even after the interview you may not have much sense of what scored points with them. So, you have to spread your bets.

You have personal interests. You can demonstrate that. You also need to demonstrate that work and career interests are of great importance to you.

Controversial or Time-Consuming Activities

If you have interests that your interviewer shares, these common interests can promote rapport and identification. The best thing that can happen in an interview is that the interviewer begins to bond with you.

When you're interviewing for jobs, try to go to the office and meet the people you'll be working with. Ask them whether they organize social activities or spend time together outside of the workplace. You'll be spending eight hours or more with them, five days a week, so you'd better be sure you feel compatible with them.

—Donya Levine, age 22

Compatibility counts because it promotes teamwork and commitment, and if compatibility is not established in the first interview, you have missed a key opportunity.

But be very careful about how you establish compatibility. Don't assume that because your interviewer works at a conservative investment banking company that she will share your conservative religious beliefs. Don't assume the young, easygoing recruiter from the start-up software company will be turned on by your commitment to the American Civil Liberties Union.

One of the worst things that can happen at an interview is that the interviewer identifies you with a group or a point of view that he detests. Here again, he won't be wearing a sign explaining his belief system. But instead of spreading these bets, you want to keep them off the table.

You may have spent spring vacation helping at Planned Parenthood. You may have been busy picketing abortion clinics. In general, you have much more to lose than to gain by making this information available to recruiters. Most employers don't want controversy or fistfights at the water cooler. Keep your opinions, whether religious, political, or social, out of the picture, starting with your résumé. There is no requirement that you list everything you did, or even everything you were heavily involved with. As a practical matter, if you don't bring up some of what you do and are, then recruiters won't know about it. You may want to be selective in what you put forward. There's no prize for letting it all hang out.

> *My hobby is playing the stock market. I do it in a small way, and I do well at it. I mentioned this to one interviewer and I could see him cringe. He went on to tell me how it's really not possible to beat the market. I never brought the subject up at another interview.*

> *—Leonard, age 23*

Unless you're positive that the person interviewing you shares your particular, strong religious, political, or social convictions— and that emphasizing your common interest will help you get the job—keep your potentially controversial views and activities to yourself.

Employers prefer to hire people for whom continuing success at work is the key value, and who are unlikely to have conflicting commitments. If you're a chess champion who has participated in tournaments around the country and even abroad, that is a nice accomplishment. So is growing prize-winning orchids. But these things can tend to make you a less desirable rather than a more desirable employee, because they threaten to distract you from or even to take you physically away from your work. If you mention such things at all, you need to do so in a way that reduces their apparent potential for conflict with your commitment to the job.

Developing Oral Communication Skills

In the end, a prospective employer is going to judge you primarily on what you say in interviews. The effectiveness of what you say will depend on your oral communication skills. No matter what job and career you want, these skills are of pivotal importance in getting you started.

Some jobs leverage oral communication skills more heavily than others do, but almost all of them require effective listening and speaking. You need to ask about your tasks, engage the assistance of others, and report your problems and results. Later, to advance beyond the entry level, you will need to lead and guide others, and persuade and teach them. None of this works if you're tongue-tied or simply hate to talk when more than one person is listening. Here is how it looks from outside the college walls:

I am realizing more and more that the ability to talk is one of the important skills I can master for my job. That skill allows me to talk my way through a phone call with a client when I really have no idea what is going on. The debating I did in college has served me well.

—*Michael Bernstein, age 24*

You may not want a job like Michael's, where you have to talk even when you "really have no idea of what is going on." But at a minimum, you will have to be willing to step forward without hesitation and speak out on the many occasions when you do know what you're talking about. Otherwise, the value of what you know will be lost—to others and therefore to you yourself.

Participating in debates is one way to get comfortable with speaking to an audience, but it's not the only way. Lawrence Tribe is now a professor at the Harvard Law School and has argued cases before the U.S. Supreme Court. When he was an undergraduate, he was a star debater, but he seldom missed any other opportunity to talk and argue. He probably could have gotten along without the formal debating. But for a person who has not developed the habit of talking to strangers and trying to persuade them, debating is one natural way to turn on capabilities that most of us have, but that many of us suppress, often because of shyness and lack of confidence.

A course in public speaking can be helpful. Involvement in student politics can be helpful. You will have many alternatives. Few of us are born articulate, pithy, and convincing, and most of us arrive at college without strong public speaking skills. Make sure you take them home with you.

The ability to express oneself clearly both orally and in writing is much more important than knowing a bunch of programming languages. I'd much rather hire someone who has taken a writing seminar or who speaks fluent French . . . .

—*Roy Levin, Director, Systems Research Center, Digital Equipment Corporation*

The Whole Package

As long as you have a high degree of curiosity and energy and a penchant for action, you will find your place.

—*John Pepper, CEO of Procter & Gamble*

Is this CEO looking for passive people, for people who do no more than follow rules and instructions? Evidently not. Just the opposite.

> People who make hiring decisions are not usually inscrutable or illogical. With a minimum of orientation and background, you can largely predict how they will think and judge. Their judgment will be based on what they see and hear. What they see and hear will be up to you.

Recruiters are charged with the responsibility for judging who is most likely to do the best on the job. This is not, in the end, a matter of checking off boxes. They won't require you to have one success on a team, one other extracurricular leadership role, and one big dollop of generosity, for example. On the contrary, what you did outside of class, wherever you did it, will be judged in terms of what it revealed about your likely contribution on the job. The question is not, "Is this a good person?" but rather, "Will this person do well for us?"

Employers are looking for evidence that you will perform for them. Favorable factors are: conspicuous success in any endeavor, especially ones that involve working with people and that demonstrate initiative or effectiveness in implementing changes. Your effectiveness in presenting yourself and your achievements is crucial. Unfavorable factors are: failures, lack of consistent focus, and any propensity for distraction or for commitment to interests, including activities or values, that could conflict with job performance.

How Can Your Work Experience Help?

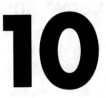

Second only to formal class work, job experience is the most important activity for many students during their college years. It's also the first or second most important factor (after academic performance) in judging candidates for employment.

In the most recent Employer Benchmark Survey conducted by the National Association of Colleges and Employers, work and internship experience ranked slightly above GPA as the number-two factor used in prescreening candidates.

For recruitment through the Internet, professional experience and skills can be so important that they outweigh GPA:

> *When companies recruit on the Internet, some don't choose to use GPA in their criteria. They consider skills and professional experience to be much more important. This is entirely different from what happens when a placement office sends a recruiter a ton of résumés.*

> *—Rachel Bell, cofounder, JobDirect.com*

Converting Necessity to Opportunity

The desire to gain professional experience is by no means the only or even the most important reason students work. For many, work is a necessity because grants, loans, and contributions by their families can't cover tuition and living expenses. Some have children or parents to support. Since every hour spent working is taken away from studying, students in this situation have very good reason to seek the highest paying job available. It may often seem that the highest paying job you can find has little to contribute to your career, or even that the need to take such a job is keeping you from getting internships or other professional experience that would help you more later.

> Your employer defines the requirements of your job. You define its opportunities. If your employer is insistent on viewing you as only one of the cogs in his machine, then you may need to look for better opportunities elsewhere. But most employers want to do better, and they are receptive to practical ideas and additional effort from good workers.

Your imagination and initiative can turn almost any job into an experience that will bring you credit on your résumé and in your interviews.

> *I worked behind the counter at a dry cleaner's. I saw a lot of clothes coming in that needed repairs—ranging from loose buttons to seams and stains—and I convinced them to offer "guaranteed ready to wear" cleaning at a higher price. It was a big success, and nothing I did interested my interviewers more than that.*
>
> *—Chuck, age 23*

Night janitorial work sounds terrible, but I figured out how they could satisfy clients better while reducing man hours worked. This got me into methods and quality engineering, and a very satisfying career.

—Neil, University of Nevada, age 24

Neil never had to put "janitor" on his résumé. He included the name of his employer and a synopsis of his accomplishments.

Take the Highest Paying Job? Or the One with Greatest Career Potential?

Even if you don't need to maximize your income, this income may still be very important to you. The job that will make you the most money probably won't be the job that can contribute the most to launching your career. How do you choose between the job with the greatest career potential and the one that will pay the most right now? It depends on your needs and priorities.

I was absolutely determined not to leave college saddled with a lot of debt. I worked for the money, and apart from that I focused on grades. I wound up with a fine job, and I'm my own woman.

—Judy, age 24

Students have varying reasons for wanting to avoid student loans. These can range from a wish to leave possibilities open for making low-income choices after college, to moral and purely psychological considerations. If debt makes you very unhappy, then you probably shouldn't incur debt.

Judy satisfied her priorities from the top down. She made do without job experience that could have helped her learn more about what she wanted or didn't want to do when she graduated, and also could have helped her qualify for jobs. For Judy, this may turn out to be no sacrifice at all, but it's hard to be confident of such a result in advance. Here's another point of view:

> *I've been willing to invest in my future—after all, my parents have! I consider my college jobs to be a key part of my education. The pay is secondary. I've not only learned a lot about what I want to do, but I've learned about how to do it well.*
>
> *—Kevin, age 22*

Kevin borrowed, but he's confident of paying his loan back without strain. He knows that he's going to be working and earning soon. If he decided to go on straight to graduate study, his loan repayments would be deferred accordingly.

Judy and Kevin differ in their perspectives and preferences. In college and afterwards, some of the most important learning is about the things that make you miserable or happy. The more sensitive you are to the need for this learning, and the more you're willing to seek and use it, the better the insurance you will have against making decisions that violate your own desires and interests.

If you don't have an urgent need for money, don't just sit on your duff and eat bonbons. Count yourself lucky—not because you're a lady or gentleman of leisure, but because you have some flexibility in choosing part-time jobs and internships. Decisions about how much and what kind of work to do during college are among the most important that you will make, because these decisions will affect your opportunities for employment after college.

The internship and extracurricular experiences I'd had while in college were a key factor in my success during my first job search. I was 22 and had five jobs on my résumé. Someone out of college who has nothing on his résumé but a degree will be at a huge disadvantage in his first job search.

—Greg Heilmann, age 24

Decisions about jobs and internships are particularly difficult if you need to trade off the immediate financial rewards of a job against its likely value and relevance to your longer term plans. Short-term considerations can easily dominate your choices.

I temped during my summers at college because I could make the most money doing that. If I could do my college years over again, I would definitely do internships over the summers and use them to help me figure out what exactly I wanted to do upon graduation.

—Lara, age 26

Some students don't feel they need to learn about fields they are considering entering, or any other field.

I worked after school and summers from around the age of 14, and always had to earn the money for my own clothes and incidentals. I never thought of the jobs as anything other than a way to make money, and went on that way through college. I have no regrets.

—Helen, age 23

Helen went straight on from college to medical school. She's unusually poised and mature, and she seems like the kind of person who could do well in quite a number of careers. But, how much choice did she give herself—how much did she know about other work and its long-term potential, when she opted for medicine? By her own account, she chose her jobs so as to make as much money as possible, paying little attention to the possibility that job experience could illuminate her choice of occupation.

Helen's college jobs included waitressing, modelling, and working in the office of her father's construction business. She saw none of them as having any career possibilities for her. But these jobs generally paid more than she could have made in the hospital or other health care jobs that might have been available to her, or in jobs related to her other interests, including psychology and social welfare.

There are at least two ways of looking at Helen's choices. If she was totally committed to medicine from the beginning, then she had little to lose by taking jobs that did almost nothing to enhance her understanding either of medical or nonmedical careers. If, however, Helen had talents, interests, and needs that might just as well have carried her in a different direction, then she may have locked herself into a premature choice of profession by failing to use her working time to learn more both about medicine and about alternative careers.

Here is a quite different job history:

> *I was sure I wanted to be a lawyer until I did a summer of paralegal work. Then I focused on my interest in international government, and had a job working for a unit of the U.N. in Africa. The problems were awesome. I finally decided on veterinary school.*

—*Margaret, age 24*

Unhappiness with a job in your chosen field can naturally lead to your reconsidering your choice. Should you regard that possibility as a hazard or as an opportunity? Probably the latter. If the work is not going to suit you, then you're much better off learning this sooner rather than later, so that you can adjust your decisions and plans accordingly. Of course, there is some risk that your career direction will change for insubstantial or barely relevant reasons.

In Margaret's case, it seems possible that she was simply uncomfortable with working in large organizations. In such an organization, you may feel that your efforts are poorly utilized and rarely come to any visible fruition. If that is the case, perhaps Margaret will be happier as a veterinarian. But although she likes animals and has visited vets, she has never worked in a veterinary practice. If she had spent a summer doing this, Margaret might have changed her mind yet again. For instance, she might have found the demands and emotions of pet owners extremely trying. This is not to say that she's an unusually picky consumer of careers, but rather that there's a danger in favoring what you have not actually tried over what you have tried. It would be better to have a hands-on feel for what happens in a veterinary office before rather than after entering veterinary school.

Trying various jobs and internships won't guarantee that you will find the career that is ideal for you. There are too many possibilities for you to ever be able to try most of them. But it helps to investigate the option that appeals to you before heading in that direction. Better still, try jobs that will make you better informed about two or three reasonable career alternatives.

An internship points you in a potential career direction. But if you decide after the internship that you have no interest in that direction, it's OK. I interned at a mutual fund company during a summer and realized afterwards that I wasn't interested in that line of work.

—Andrew Ackerman, age 26

Some hiring managers are stuck on GPA, but relevant work experience is a must. A good GPA means the candidate is a good student. In a corporate environment, there's not much opportunity for studying. Good work experience, on the other hand, directly correlates with success in the workplace.

—Eric Hutcherson, manager of college and diversity relations, Lotus Development Corporation

Being good at studying and passing tests is not, in itself, much use to an employer. Finding ways to get good work experience while in college is a serious challenge for every student who wants or may want to go from college to a job.

Any challenging job you take during college that lets you demonstrate accomplishment can help you get the position you want when you graduate.

Finding a Job During College

There are two basic ways of looking for a job. One is to scan the market broadly to see what is available. You can do this by looking at bulletin boards, want ads, and the Internet, and possibly going to the college office responsible for helping with casual and summer employment. You will also, of course, want to make the most intensive possible use of your parents and other contacts who may be able to help with job referrals. This approach is essentially passive, and not a lot of work.

> *My uncle told me about a friend of his who worked at Saatchi. I gave him a call. We played phone tag for a couple of months but I persisted and he finally scheduled a time to meet with me. A day after I met with him, I had a job at Saatchi.*

—*Aaron Katz, age 25*

Among the most obvious of the job possibilities you see will be those offered at your campus. Some will be related to student aid or loan programs, and may include dining hall, library, and computer center jobs. In a way, these jobs represent a baseline. They are the jobs you may wind up with if you can't find anything that suits you better. Unless your career ambitions tend towards librarianship, catering, or computer stores, you will seek a job outside the college that is closer to your career target.

A disadvantage of campus jobs is that some employers will see them as part of your deal with your college, generously aimed at helping you survive, rather than as plums plucked in the competitive marketplace. It will be to your advantage to be seen as having found or created an opportunity, rather than as having merely accepted an assignment, or even an obligation. Campus jobs that in fact are open to all and must be competed for may attract some of this negative aura.

> *I had to compete like crazy to get a job as a resource person at our campus computer center. But when interviewers asked about it, some of them thought it was just a disguised form of financial aid. Was I mad!*

—*Ellie, age 25*

The second strategy for finding a job is not focused on scanning all the jobs available in the college and outside. Rather, the idea is to be proactive, to figure out what kind of job you would like to have, with what employer, and then set out to make it happen. This strategy is much more labor intensive than the first one. Even if pursued single-mindedly, it's not certain to get you the job you want. But if it succeeds, working back from your goal to a way to reach that goal can give you a much better result, in more ways than one.

> *I couldn't find an internship for the summer after my freshman year, so I was particularly determined to get one my sophomore year. That fall, I went to talk to the people on campus recruiting seniors for full-time positions. A few of them let me set up informal interviews with them. I followed those interviews with letters to make them remember me. With a bit of determination and persistence, I ended up with a great summer internship.*

—*Chris Kastensmidt, age 23*

Chris was obviously not an expert on any of the companies with which he had those first informal interviews. But he emerged from the crowd of job candidates through his initiative in seeking out the recruiters, and because of his obvious enthusiasm and determination to get an internship. Not all the interviewers were impressed—only a few. But that was enough.

Often, an opportunity simply entails taking what you have observed working well in one place and transplanting it to another place.

> *In my home town, the banks really chase students to get them as customers. But the banks near my campus were much less aggressive. I went around to all three of the nearby ones and suggested a program to get students as customers. One of them*

agreed and hired me. If only they had paid me according to results!
But this experience paid off in spades at interview time.

—Molly, age 22

Even if none of the banks had wanted to launch a program to acquire student accounts, they might well have wanted to hire interested and enthusiastic students such as Molly.

A favorite interview question is, "How did you happen to do that?" As the recruiter, would you favor the student who said, "Well, I was walking down the street and saw the sign"? Or would you prefer the one who explained how he had decided what he wanted and how he had, in effect, made his own opportunity? Probably the latter, because practical, self-starting people are very valuable to an employer.

The Pros and Cons of Parental Connections

Sometimes, the discussion of how you got a job can become much more specific—and even insulting:

You will have bad interviews. One interviewer pointed to each of
my job experiences and asked, "Did your daddy get you that job?"

—Donya Levine, age 22

Maybe this interviewer was just doing his job, learning more about the candidate. More likely, he had a chip on his shoulder about kids whose parents give them certain advantages. It won't come off well in any interview for you to blurt out, or to admit, "Well, my father got me that job," (or even your Uncle Fred, or your hairdresser). Better to get credit for making your own way.

Does this mean that you should avoid seeking out or accepting a job that is known or available to you through your parents or through someone else that you know? No. It's the visible result that counts. Having a good job and good experience counts. Good performance counts. But be aware that you may be asked how you got the job. Make sure that your answer won't get you into trouble or detract from your credibility.

You may be treated differently on a job obtained through family or other connections. In the worst case, an employer may feel that he has done enough in providing a nominal position (and a résumé line), and that there's no need to give you meaningful work to do. Other employees may resent your presence because they've been clued in to your connection.

> At the law firm, everyone just assumed that no college student could have gotten the job except through some kind of influence. In fact, there were a couple of others who even boasted that that was how they had gotten there. But it wasn't a problem for me, I just did the job, and was invited back.

> —Bruce, age 21

You will need to deal with any such problems realistically but diplomatically should they arise. In the best case, the employer may feel that he wants you to have an especially successful experience, and to end it with a highly favorable opinion of his company.

You may get a hint of what the employer has in mind for you when he offers and you accept the job, and you should assure that clear expectations about the job are shared. Judging from the experiences of the people interviewed for this book, a job where you have some indirect linkage with the employer is likely to turn out well.

> Don't be embarrassed or afraid to follow up on any leads that could bring you to the summer job you want. Summer and term-time employers, like those who employ graduating seniors, simply prefer to hire people that they feel they "know" in some way, or who have somehow been vouched for. There's no point in trying to frustrate this desire. Use it to your advantage.

How Will Employers React to Your Job Experience?

Employers are looking for relevant work or internship experience. Good past performance in a relevant internship or job shows that you know what you will be getting into with them. It shows some commitment to a career. It also shows that you had what it took to get over the first hurdle.

> *I definitely wish I had done a summer internship in publishing. Prior internship experience gives you a huge advantage when applying for a first job.*
>
> —*Jennifer, age 22*

In considering your internship experience, employers are likely to care first of all about how you got or how you chose your job. Indeed, what you have to say about prior job choices will imply quite a bit about how you're approaching your current task of getting your first "real" job. If you have been careless before, this could happen again. If you were dissatisfied before, it may happen again. If you can't be trusted to pick a job where you will be successful and happy, then you're a poor choice for the job the employer is trying to fill. You need to be able to see and highlight what you accomplished for your employer and yourself in each position that you choose to put on your résumé.

The job offer will generally go to the person seen as surest to deliver the best performance. Your job experience can provide a basis for confidence that you are that person, particularly if one or more of your jobs was similar in content or was in the same company as the one you seek to win. However, the employer needs to have confidence that you are also going to be willing and able to carry through successfully with whatever you start.

> *Somehow it worked out that I spent each of three summers with the three major auto companies, primarily in finance. When it came to hiring in senior year, each of the three seemed to have questions about my commitment.*
>
> —Anthony, age 22

Objectively, if you are going into the auto industry, it's probably a very fine thing to have a sense of the prevailing attitudes at those companies. But the company where you worked two years ago is going to be insulted that you didn't come back. In some industries, managers are particularly sensitive to issues of corporate loyalty. They are concerned that you will learn from them and then carry that learning to a competitor.

You also need to be alert to the implications of spreading your experience widely across industries. A person who has spent the last three summers in supermarket management, local government, and banking could be seen as vacillating, or thoughtless. He's going off in all directions. Yet, probing in several different directions can provide you with valuable insights. The key is being able to explain what you have done in a coherent, positive way.

> *I had great summer jobs while in college, one at the* Wall Street Journal *and one at the State Department. Still, each time I came away thinking those jobs weren't for me. That knowledge was useful in itself.*
>
> —*Senior investment banker, bulge bracket firm*

In this situation, you might prefer to de-emphasize some of your experience on your résumé, using different forms of the résumé as appropriate to different employers. There's no requirement that the résumé you submit be the same for all prospective employers.

The expectation is that you will use successive periods of work to tighten up your choice of employer, rather than to pursue long shots. The summer after your junior year is a crucial stepping stone. Many companies offer regular jobs to those who do well in such summer employment.

> *We have a 100 percent commitment by upper management to use our intern program as the number one feeder. In 1997, 82 percent of our full-time sales trainee positions were filled by the previous year's interns.*
>
> —*Jim Gwinn, Director of Global Staffing, American Cyanamid Company.*

Interns are the highest-priority candidates to be considered for employment after graduation because the company has already invested in selecting and training them. You may be able to work your way up to this preferred position in the hiring queue through less formal work with the company.

For me, it was first just a summer job, picked more or less as a target of opportunity. Then I began to think of them as a place to go back to, it was comfortable. Finally, it felt like a result rather than a decision.

—Eric, age 22

Working an internship can be like getting friendly with the girl or boy next door. Before you know it, the assumptions made by families and neighbors are getting stronger and stronger, and you would have to kick and scream to refute them. But you won't kick and scream, because it's not all that bad, and you're a nice person.

The company I've worked for since college has a training program at my school. I sort of fell into the trap of going through with the training, as I was feeling the pressures of needing to get a job right away and I knew that only large companies come to campus to recruit. Thinking back, I wish I had taken more time to explore my options. I might well be happier in my job today if I had taken that time.

—Michael Bernstein, age 24

The plus side of intensive and continuing involvement with a single employer is that you know very well what you're getting into. The minus side is that you fixate on a target that blots out all other possibilities. Maybe you could have found another company, another industry or another location that would give you a better fit and more positive prospects, at least over the long term.

Look again from the recruiter's side of the desk:

> *During each college summer, I worked at a medium-sized bank in St. Louis. But I could see as a senior that when I interviewed for jobs outside of banking, the recruiters were really skeptical. They assumed I would end up going into banking.*
>
> *—Jessie, age 23*

Is that a surprise? Recruiters are generally logical rather than whimsical, and they interpret minimum evidence in straightforward, predictable ways. You will be seeing a lot of them, so it's better to focus on their common characteristics rather than on an occasional exception. When the oral and the retained written word conflict, recruiters have a tendency to give greater credence to the written word. And the most likely reason anyone would return so loyally to the same employer is because she intended to stick with that employer, or at least to go with a similar employer for the long term.

Your work experience can easily typecast you. Interviewers know that it's very little trouble for a student to sign up for a lot of interviews. They are wary of wasting their time and offers on people who interview just for practice or to learn about the company. If your CV, specifically your work history, suggests to a normal person that you're headed straight for

something different from what you're interviewing for, then you need both to adjust your résumé and to be proactive in addressing the issue.

When it comes to going back to the same summer employer or the same industry, you will need to reflect carefully. It's surely riskier to jump into something you don't know than to recommit to something you know and like. But there are also risks in turning a good summer job into a career. Day-to-day convenience, lack of stress, and decent pay won't necessarily produce career satisfaction. You don't want to be like the couple that lived together happily for three years, but began to have problems as soon as they got married. Some things feel fine as long as they are perceived as provisional, but become uncomfortable once stamped with the seal of permanency.

Your work experiences also establish a pedigree that is read as a reflection of your qualities and desirability. Interesting jobs with prestige employers suggest that you're first rate.

> *Having a pedigree helps a lot. I tried to set the stage around me so that every academic and professional experience I had was the best it could be.*
>
> *—Heidi Horner, VP New Business Development, Athena Neurosciences*

Employment During the School Year

Local term-time employment possibilities are far more limited than summer job alternatives, even if your campus is located in or near a major city. You don't have much time to waste commuting, and the limited hours of working time you have to offer may not be sufficient to enable you to have an ongoing role in any activity that is not quite routine. A great many companies want summer interns, but far fewer want part-time interns during the school year. Imagination and initiative can work wonders.

> *I proposed a project that had me visiting the different stores and surveying their displays and sales practices. They bought the idea because they thought I resembled their typical customer.*

> *—Marcia, age 21*

Your summer employer, if you had a good job and a good relationship, is likely to be your preferred term-time employer—even if the work during the term has to be done at a distance. This is true because your summer job is much more likely to have professional content than will any job you can get for the term, starting from scratch with a new employer.

Although it's easiest to create an interesting term-time opportunity by working from knowledge and relationships gained during summer work, there are other possibilities:

> *In a computer science course, I did a project comparing the performance of search engines. Then I went to one of the search engine companies and proposed carrying this work further. It was a good bargain for them, and they bought it.*

> *—Richard, age 20*

Richard's experience shows how it may be possible to arrange term-time employment even with geographically distant companies. Using E-mail, communication in real time is equally practical and cheap whether it's going across the street or across the country. Richard's example also shows how course assignments (and in some cases, a professor's contacts) can be turned into employment opportunities.

Sometimes, employment in a more standard—and hence competitive—setting can also provide very strong evidence of a student's work value. This is true particularly when the employment is carried far enough to demonstrate real talent and achievement.

> *I had done some telemarketing in high school. At college, I went around to the local telemarketing shops and asked what it would take for me to become a night supervisor. They said all the supervisors were college graduates. But in two years, I attained my goal.*
>
> —*Jack, age 22*

Jack didn't point it out, but his GPA is flirting with 2.0. That is not because he spends so much time on his telemarketing. He has just never been all that interested in cracking books and acing tests. Yet Jack had absolutely no difficulty getting several excellent job offers when he graduated—and they didn't all involve telemarketing.

Don't ever lose sight of the fact that what recruiters want is women and men who will perform well, and the best proof that you will perform well is not GPA or athletic achievement, but actual job performance.

Jack is a hot property, not because he has specific skills in telemarketing, but because he has been recognized as doing excellent work over a long period of time. He has demonstrated ambition, consistency, and results.

Letters of recommendation from former bosses are unlikely to count for much in themselves. They are often exaggerated and difficult to confirm. Promotions and raises, however, are more likely to establish the value of your work. The best thing a job can do for you is to provide strong evidence of your ability to perform. It can also give you a view of what you will be facing if you move into a particular job environment after graduation.

> *I found the real-life experience I gained in the lab I worked in during college particularly useful. I learned about what the general atmosphere in scientific research would be like: competitive and hard work.*
>
> *—Heidi Horner, VP of Business Development, Athena Neourosciences*

In entry-level jobs, highly specialized know-how is rarely of great importance. If you had what it takes to do outstanding work in one such job, you will be considered ready to do the same in many others. For instance, telemarketing and supervising telemarketers may sound very technical and exotic. But if you can do that, you can sell. And you can supervise and train almost any group of telephone service personnel.

When you have to make a fresh start to find work for the school year, think about how to identify the companies you want to work with. Then think about tasks that would have value to them and that would actually leverage your unusual situation—the fact that you're a part timer and a student. This can be anything from shift work, as in telemarketing, to a project requiring independent compilation and analysis of data. Anything the company can get out of such an independent project will be ridiculously cheap compared to hiring a consultant or using an outside firm. Their primary concern won't be the cost. They are more likely to worry about any coordination or other burdens your project imposes on their management and operations.

> *I knew someone in a company that had begun to face heavy competition in the mail. I offered to assemble and analyze mailings by competitors. They bought the idea.*
>
> *—Becky, age 21*

You may think some of these interviewees are extraordinary. You may find it hard to imagine how you could possibly do what they did. Well, you probably can't do exactly what any of them did. But after all, Becky almost surely could not have done what Richard or Jack or Marcia did, or vice versa. You have your own profile of interests, needs, and points of contact. Draw inspiration and understanding from these success stories, and apply them to your own circumstances.

How Much Is Enough?

How much you work while in college may be determined by your financial needs, or by your preference for learning about and performing in jobs. However, there can be many other conflicting demands on your time, including both formal and less formal studies, extracurriculars, and vacation travel and other family activities. So, how much work is enough?

> *We look for the best of the best. We see candidates with résumés that look like they've been working in the industry for ten years. It's a*

competitive market. My advice: Intern at big-time companies and do good work.

—Eric Hutcherson, Manager of College and Diversity Relations, Lotus Development Corporation

Not every employer is so demanding. What counts is the output, not the input. Working through every summer vacation and many hours each week of the term will demonstrate energy and conviction, but these can be equally well shown in many other ways. The various other benefits you can get from working while in college can be important. These include a stronger recruiting profile and a more developed and confident conception of what you want to do after college, as well as current income that can make your college life more pleasant. How much effort it's worth putting in to pursue these good results depends both on your opportunities and on your success in your work.

Successful job seekers vary greatly in how much they have worked at college. No work at all is certainly not enough, if you want to work right after college. Employers have a right to expect that you prove your ability to perform a job before coming to them for a permanent position. It will be difficult to explain why your need for additional course work, travel, or some other activity was always of higher priority.

> You don't need athletics in order to get hired, and you don't have to have done much for your college or community. But you better have worked.

With some of the interviewers, it seemed like they were rolling their eyes. How could I now be looking for a job for the first time ever? I found it was better to just get past that issue rather than try to explain.

—Jeffrey, age 22

For this purpose, summer employment is enough. With a couple of carefully chosen and successful summer jobs, you may not need to do any work during the term that is oriented towards getting you positioned for the right job after graduation. A great many employers, like other people, feel it's better not to spend a lot of hours working during the school term if you can afford not to do so.

What If the Job Is Not Working Out?

Many students, like other employees, have had bad experiences at work. Experiences like these may seem to result from incompetent or prejudiced supervisors, or employers who don't make good on their promises, or on incompatibilities between themselves and the job requirements. These are not things that any prospective employer wants to hear about.

I spend a lot of my interview time listening either to bragging or to excuses. The excuses are worse. "Just the facts, m'am."

—Barry, corporate recruiter, age 33

Actually, recruiters will get only a selection of the facts, and it's up to you to make that selection. You won't have the same luxury after your first job, because in subsequent interviews you will be asked to explain how you spent your years and months from graduation up to the current date. But because not all college students work every term and every summer, you will have much more flexibility while pursuing your first job. You don't have to mention—even in your résumé—any experience that won't be helpful in making your case.

Employers are looking for people who persevere no matter how serious the unpleasantness and difficulties. They are certainly not looking for quitters, nor for people who think that excuses can justify failure or poor performance. Make your working time count for you.

> *Two summers ago, I saw right away that my employer wasn't going to have enough for me to do. My roommate's employer had too much for him to do. So, I switched. And I'm glad I did. It's only the second employer on my résumé.*
>
> *—Phillip, age 22*

Phillip's decision enabled him to have a more productive summer and a better work history to present to employers. Apart from your earnings, you have little to gain by twiddling your thumbs in a nonproductive situation. A job that can't be made to work out for you probably won't produce great results from the employer's standpoint, either.

Are You Developing Practical Skills?

Many students worry, particularly if they have majored in a liberal arts subject such as English or history, that they will leave college not knowing how to do any job at all, even though they expect to need and get a job when they graduate. Yet if you graduated with a degree in mechanical engineering or business administration, you likewise would not have been trained for and would not be qualified for any particular job. You would need to learn more and would also require some specific training before you could apply your college learnings productively to any particular position in an organization.

You're probably aware that high schoolers are hired by McDonald's seemingly irrespective of whether they have ever lifted a finger in the family kitchen, or ever had a job serving food or cashiering purchases. In a way, the principle is the same. It's certainly not true that just anyone can do the job, but the requirements for the job actually relate to some fairly general qualities and capabilities rather than to highly specific job skills. For instance, a person who can't arrive on time, pay attention to the job, dress properly, stay clean, and speak correctly and politely won't survive at McDonald's. But to get hired you don't have to come in knowing how to operate the fryer. They expect to teach you things like that after you begin the job.

Thus, your first focus should be on developing and demonstrating skills that are of fundamental and broad importance to successful work, rather than on learning the mechanics of specific jobs. Many people lose out on job opportunities, or perform poorly once they are hired, because they lack these core skills. Identification of key work skills and the means by which you can acquire them will be the main focus of this chapter. There's more to learn, and more to get excited about doing, than can easily be compressed into four years.

> *Make use of every day at school. I wish I had gotten up earlier every morning and used each day to its fullest.*

—*John, age 25*

You will see that most of the skills you need can't be acquired merely by doing well in classes, whether those classes are in English or in aeronautical engineering. Work experience, and to some extent successful involvement in student activities, can help you build and display these skills. In deciding how to allocate your time and what to do in your jobs and activities, it's important to be aware of the skills you will need in your work so that you can aim to acquire them.

Can You Do What You're Told?

The disappointments and failures that college students and recent graduates commonly have with jobs often occur because young workers simply are not used to doing the things they are told to do, and in the way they are told to do them.

Of course, I'd had little jobs where I just did what I was told. But when I began to work after graduation, I was shocked. I'm used to discussing things, to being invited to suggest ideas. But my boss just wanted me to follow instructions and not talk up.

—Carol, age 23

To put it simply, you often don't have to do as you're asked in college. The professor says to read a book, but you might not read it . . . or at least not when she says to read it.

> Work is often more like your image of the army than it's like college or home. When the boss asks you nicely to do it, you must do it, rather than argue or delay or ignore the request. If you don't have that practical skill, namely the skill of doing as you're told, then you are likely to have a very hard time at work.

I'm used to asking "Why?" Not out of curiosity, but to understand the goal and the reasons. At first, my boss was patient with this but I could see that she was getting increasingly testy about it, so I just stopped. It was hard.

—Martin, age 23

Asking "Why?" can be read as a challenge: "Give me a good reason for what you just told me to do!" Any decent boss knows that you're better off understanding the task at hand rather than just following orders blindly. But he may be offended by the style and timing of your questions, and he may be upset by the implication that you won't act until you're convinced he's right. Very likely he will feel that he simply doesn't have time to transfer to you the whole framework of experience and reasoning that underlies his decisions. In his view, it's up to him to decide when and in what form it is worthwhile and timely for him to give you the "why," and until then, it's not a subject to discuss.

So, how can you learn the practical skill of simply doing as you are told? How can you gain and justify confidence in your ability to carry out requests and instructions without selectivity or second guessing? The best way is surely by working, so that you gain exposure to the demands of a job situation and become accustomed to meeting those demands. Sometimes what you're asked to do will seem irrelevant or stupid. Sometimes it will be necessary for you to find a polite, constructive way to let the boss know he's clearly wrong. But in general, you will need to learn how to suspend or dampen your critical side so that you become an implementer rather than a filter.

Some jobs are better than others for obtaining the necessary experience. Neither a completely routine job that you do over and over, nor a unique and highly independent job will do the best for you in this respect. You need a more typical job, where the boss will give you considerable direction from time to time and you will need to follow it.

> *The job I found most useful was as a sales assistant in an insurance office. I made sure that what had to be done got done, but in addition I was able to suggest and implement some really valuable enhancements to our sales and service systems.*
>
> *—Monica, age 23*

Figuring Out What the Boss Wants

It may seem easy to do what you're told to do, though for many of us it really is not. A more complex problem, and an even more common one, arises when you're not actually told what to do. You are merely given a sketch of one or more objectives or one or more methods or strategies. Then you're expected to make your decisions and allocate your efforts so that you carry out the right method and get the desired results.

Compare that to what happens in college. Each course has a syllabus and requirements. At the end, there is an exam. You may have a lot of other things you want to learn, but in any case you must do well enough on the exam. Your information on what will be covered by the exam is incomplete and, to some extent, contradictory. This can and often does lead students to do nothing, or almost nothing, at least for a while.

The problem you face in many jobs is much more complex. There is no exam, nor any homework. Feedback is sparse. Yet somehow what you produce, or your overall performance, is going to be graded, and you're then going to be rewarded or punished accordingly.

> *She told me to be nice to customers on the phone, so I was. They were watching what I did, but afterwards they said I made too many of the adjustments that customers asked for. As if I were a weakling, or as if the customers were paying me off or something!*

> —*Dennis, age 24*

Often, the objectives you must achieve are complex, or at least they can't be measured on a single scale, such as the number of widgets produced. In Dennis' case, he has to deal with as many customers as possible. He has to satisfy those customers. And yet, he's not supposed to give too many of them an adjustment, or refund. That is not at all like college, where you just add up the points for the exam or for the course, and assign the grade accordingly.

It would have been very nice if Dennis's boss had given him numerical standards or limits to be honored. He might have said, "You'll be doing fine if you handle eight customers per hour, you don't annoy more than ten percent of them, and you don't give refunds to more than five percent." But goals and standards often are not so specific. Supervision proceeds on an exception basis. You find out what you should have achieved by being told about your shortfalls. This can be upsetting, and it can seem very unfair.

Learning how to do what the boss wants, or what he will praise and reward, is much more complicated than merely doing specifically as you're told. In some instances, the boss may not really know what he requires, or his goals may change while the work is in progress. He may give you an idealized or oversimplified version of what is really going to matter to him, perhaps because he doesn't know any better. You learn how to recognize and cope with these problems through experience.

My boss told me to get and keep all our old stock of books marked up to current prices. That would not have been practical, but I accomplished his purpose by changing to a system where the prices were updated in the system rather than on the books themselves.

—Ryan, age 23

Relevant experience can include work that you do while in college. It can also include other activities in which you play a subordinate role, such as clubs and sports. The frustrations can be painful.

> *How was I supposed to know that it did more harm than good to increase the output by 10 percent if in doing so I increased the scrap by 2 percent? I only found out after it was too late, when I was called on the carpet and reamed out.*

—*Peter, age 24*

Peter could have found out more sooner by asking, though his knowledge would still have been incomplete. Among the most valuable of practical skills is the sense of what questions to ask, and how to deal with the answers. You don't want to be a nuisance, nor do you want to seem ignorant, but there are things you badly need to know. Identifying which things these are is of crucial importance. Some knowledge of accounting could also have helped Peter see how much he could afford to lose in scrap in order to accelerate his output.

Reading Reactions

Accepting and acting on explicit, verbal feedback can be difficult, especially if you don't like criticism, or if you feel that you have been misjudged. It's even more important to be able to read and respond to positive and negative reactions that are expressed less directly.

> *I began to tune in on how my boss and other managers reacted at meetings. To some people and some kinds of input, they reacted*

with smiles and nods. To other people and other kinds of behavior,
they tended to react with a frown, with heightened tension, with a
tapping finger or foot.

—*Robert, age 27*

It's easiest to pick up these reactions when you're an observer and the boss is reacting to someone else's input, so that you're not distracted by your own stakes in the game. Your mission is not to tell everyone what they most want to hear. Rather, you should be refining your understanding of just what it is about people and their behavior that elicits either a positive or a negative reaction from your boss. Then, you need to put that knowledge to work.

Perhaps you think it's manipulative to bend your actions consciously towards what will earn positive feedback. If that is your concern, think again. Who is manipulating whom? If your boss gets you to operate the way he wants you to by giving you direct or indirect feedback, sounds like he's manipulating you rather than the other way around. However, he is not manipulating you. He's simply doing his own job, by influencing you to do your job in the way he thinks it should be done.

My boss said that he hated conflict and competition in the
organization. Through trial and error, I learned that what he hated
were raised voices or backbiting. He didn't mind at all if people had
a frank and civilized difference of opinion about how to get the best
results, or if they tried to outdo each other.

—*Marion, age 23*

Special problems arise when you disagree with the boss. Any indication of your disagreement that is perceptible when the boss is with you in a group can endanger your relationship with the boss. Potentially, at least, you're confronting and embarrassing him. It's not like disagreeing with a professor in class (that is often dangerous enough), because the boss's effectiveness is dependent on his ability to impose his views, and he has the power to fire you. Neither is the case for your professors.

Even in a one-on-one setting, the benefits of expressing disagreement need to be weighed against the risks. The benefits include your expectation that the boss can be made to see reason and that a more realistic and effective course of action will result. You may even hope to get deserved credit for courage and persuasiveness as well as for good judgment that has improved the boss's performance or even saved the day.

The risks of disagreeing are that your outspokenness will antagonize the boss and even make him dig in his heels more firmly.

> *The boss told our group that our reports for clients needed to be longer. Afterwards, I asked him whether there might be a problem that some clients would feel we were wasting their money just churning out pages. I could see he was unhappy with me for weeks after that.*
>
> —*Alex, age 24*

By Alex's own account, his comment was confrontational. Furthermore, it has the flavor of an attempt to avoid working harder, and that is never an attractive pose to adopt. Why second guess the boss on this point? If he's wrong, that is his own problem, and the problem is unlikely to be serious.

Obtaining Cooperation and Action

A crucial practical skill that can make the difference between success and failure on the job is the skill of motivating people to do what you want them to do. Very few jobs can be performed adequately merely by pouring on personal effort. Almost all require that you influence the behavior of coworkers, customers, or others.

In college, you try to motivate teachers to give you high grades. That is a quite special form of interaction. It's not altogether different from what you have to do later in motivating your boss to give your performance a high rating. But it's quite different from what you have to do in order to get coworkers and others to do what you need done in order to achieve performance objectives.

> *Soon after starting my job, I was assigned to supervise a group of data entry clerks. Their attitude seemed to be that as long as they kept from getting fired, everything was fine. I had a heck of a time getting their attention.*

> —Claire, age 25

Evidently, this was a practical skill for which Claire's college years had left her unprepared. Perhaps she could have learned some of what she needed by exercising leadership responsibility for a college social organization or a team. But work is different, because workers are paid and their rights and obligations are determined by an employment relationship. There's no assumption that we are all in this together, voluntarily.

Many of the skills you will need to succeed on the job are most readily and surely acquired by observation and participation in a job setting. No need for elaborate theory, and no need to reinvent the wheel. See what works and adapt it to your own needs.

When I became a telemarketing supervisor, in my junior year, I had already worked under and closely observed at least six other supervisors. It wasn't a case of what I liked or what style I'd choose. My eyes and ears told me a lot about what works and what doesn't.

—*Jack, age 22*

If your first job after college is going to be bolting on fenders on an assembly line, then you can get along without knowing much about how to motivate others. But in many other jobs, you will face challenges much more complex than Jack had with his telemarketers, because you will have to motivate and influence people, such as customers or fellow workers, over whom you have no formal authority. Even formal authority can't take the place of leadership skills.

My first "job" after college was as an ensign on a naval cruiser, where I ran an office of male enlisted clerks and typists. They knew I knew nothing, so all I could do was sit there and let my subordinates, the chiefs and petty officers, run the place.

—*Stanley, age 46*

Actually, Stanley did more than "sit there." He learned from his subordinates not only about the work of the office and how to run the office, but also about leadership. They didn't lead by giving orders. That was the last resort. They led by motivating, exemplifying, teaching, persuading, and evaluating. Stanley learned a lot in the navy.

Selling

Selling involves motivating and influencing others specifically in order to get them to buy something. It's a practical skill that largely involves overcoming your own shyness and lack of confidence and becoming more assertive. No matter what you're selling, or to whom you're selling, the same capabilities apply.

> *I got a job as a freshman working for a company that sold to students. I liked the idea of commissions, but at first I hated the selling. As I got better, I started to like it. I want to get a job that will build on and leverage my selling skills.*
>
> —*Peggy, age 22*

When you get better at doing something, you start liking it better. The first few lessons on the piano or violin are a lot less fun than the playing and the lessons after you get the hang of it. The same is true for selling—or accounting. With experience and skill comes confidence, and some pride and pleasure. There are exceptions:

> *I sold knives for one or two summers during college. It wasn't the most thrilling of experiences, but it taught me that I was a terrible salesman, and that knowledge was very useful.*
>
> —*John Duff, venture capitalist*

Although not everyone wants to sell, and not everyone can be successful in selling, selling ranks high among the practical skills that students can first master in college, or even before, and then apply to getting jobs and succeeding in those jobs. It helps to start by liking what you sell.

> *Looking for a summer job, I walked into the store and told them: I love the clothes here, I need the money, and I know I'll enjoy selling. They hired me!*

> —*Jane, age 22*

Jane doesn't look like a model, and she doesn't talk like a slick salesperson. She is effective at communicating her honesty and her interest in other people. These qualities made her a success at selling clothes, and taught her that she could thrive on selling.

Before she could start selling to customers, Jane had to sell the store manager on the idea of hiring her to sell. Sounds like this was easy for her, probably because she expressed herself with enthusiasm and confidence. Those qualities have a very strong impact in a wide range of situations. In order to sell any product or concept, you have to start by selling yourself.

> *Getting a job is about more than simply having done well in college. It's all about how effectively you can market yourself and explain to interviewers why you did the things you did and how they led you to seek employment in the field.*

> —*Arnab Mishra, age 24*

When you're selling your own personal work product, the task is similar. You have to project conviction about the quality and value of your work. In fact, you have to be immodest.

I am a painter and I earn my living primarily by painting pictures for banks and other corporations of buildings that they own. It turns out to be easy to sell them on this idea, and I find the work challenging and fun.

—Mary, age 51

As an artist, Mary has developed a specialty where success is dependent on her professional skill, on her ability to give clients what they want, and also very much on her selling skills. She's a practical, down-to-earth person who has no trouble relating to corporate managers, people who are often quite uncomfortable as buyers of art. She obviously believes in what she's doing, and in the fact that paintings can help both to humanize and dignify corporate properties. Very often, Mary is able to persuade others to share these beliefs.

A creative person with less conviction about his work can have a much harder time. Suppose what you want to do after college is to write fiction. To earn a living at it, you will have to sell agents, magazine editors, and publishers just in order to get them to read what you write, to see whether they like it. Ultimately, your fiction is going to have to sell the reader on getting into it and staying with it—through your titles, opening paragraphs, tone, and style.

For two years after graduation, I lived in the basement of my mother's house, and I wrote. Of course, I never knew whether I had the talent to make it as a writer. Finally, I just gave up.

—Tom, age 36

It's possible, though it's far from certain, that Tom had plenty of talent as a writer. He might have earned a living at it, or even achieved considerable recognition. But there was something else that he lacked. He just didn't have the talent, confidence, will, and skill to sell what he wrote. If you can't sell it, then you can't get paid for it, whatever its value.

Tom's experience highlights a more general point. If you want an independent career, if you want to be self-employed, then your success is very likely to be heavily dependent on selling. After all, in a one-person office or a small group, there is not likely to be anyone else to do the selling for you. Your success, and your income, will depend on how well you sell, not just on how good a lawyer or artist you are.

> *I thought dentistry would mean using my skills in order to help people. But I've found there's a lot of selling involved. "Why do I need a crown?" "I don't mind the way that tooth looks!" "That'll hurt too much, I'd rather wait." I have to sell every day, even every hour.*
>
> *—Rebecca, age 33*

Within living memory, lawyers were not even allowed to advertise or to solicit clients, and every doctor and dentist seemed assured of making a good living in independent practice without ever having to make any marketing effort. It's not like that anymore. The dominance of market capitalism in the United States implies a greater need for selling. At the individual level, it amounts to a choice between joining an organization to earn a salary, or else accepting the importance of selling skills to your personal success and prosperity.

If you're thinking of freelance work or self-employment, then you had better start learning to sell as soon as possible. If you find you can't do it or absolutely hate it, then you will have to rethink your career objective. You can't afford to make such discoveries after you have spent years and hundreds of thousands of dollars learning your trade. Dental schools rarely have courses on sales techniques, and it's going to be inefficient and chancy to learn the selling on the job.

An increasing number of dentists, doctors, lawyers, architects, and other professionals have salaried jobs. These are primarily people who choose to avoid the uncertainties as well as the selling activities that you can't avoid facing squarely if you go into business for yourself or as a member of a small group. If you set career objectives that entail self employment, then you need to develop and test your selling and marketing skills while you're still in college. Even if you don't plan on self-employment, you need to be responsive to the need for selling inside or outside your organization. This need is more or less pivotal in the majority of jobs and careers.

> I wanted to be an architect in order to design and build beautiful and functional buildings. But you can't make a dollar without doing an awful lot of selling. If you don't enjoy turning people on with your vision and ideas, then you can't do it.

—*Nicky, Los Angeles, age 41*

Not a single person interviewed had any regrets about trying selling and learning selling skills while in college.

You can sell advertising in the school paper or you can walk through the stands at the ball game selling refreshments. Either way, you have to make a noise, you have to get people to do what you want them to do. This is not a case of "Try it and you will surely like it." It is, instead, a case of "Try it because you will have to do it later, and once you have tried it, you will understand and do it better."

Adapting and Demonstrating Versatility

The most important practical skill that can be learned is the skill of adapting to the requirements and possibilities of a work situation. Even a baby has habits, and as you get older you acquire more and more of them. These habits can filter what you see, limit what you do, and make you inept at adjusting your own behavior so as to get the job done right.

> *My most disappointing hire was Rita, a woman who was very bright, with outstanding interpersonal skills. But whatever I wanted her to do, it came out "her way." She never figured out anything about what I wanted.*

> *—Lilly, age 37*

This was not a case of unwillingness to carry out instructions, nor was Lilly vague about what she wanted Rita to do. The problem was Rita's inability to get outside and beyond herself enough to recognize that what Lilly wanted was actually somewhat different from what Rita's own habits and assumptions would generate. To Rita, what she was doing was just common sense; it was the only possible way of carrying out Lilly's requests and instructions. But it wasn't adaptive and it wasn't adequate. After less than a year, Lilly helped Rita find another job outside the company.

One reason why many employers favor students who have dealt successfully with a number of widely different situations is that such behavior shows adaptation. Special skills and special interests are by no means a negative. It's multiplicity and diversity of interests and achievements that is a positive. A student who has done very well in a number of diverse subjects is also attractive to hire, because he's likely to be highly adaptive, whether or not he's highly intelligent. If you can do only one or a few things well, then it seems unlikely that very many of the things your employer needs done will be among those you're good at.

> Demonstrated versatility implies the adaptability you will need to do a job that is bound to change and evolve.

Recent years have demanded massive and wrenching changes in companies and business practices. The pace of change seems to be accelerating, with deregulation, downsizing, globalization, and the rapid implementation of new technologies. Virtually no industry or company is exempt, even the most staid and conservative. The typical employer wants to hire a woman or man who can rapidly master the first job and who can evolve to meet changing and unpredictable organizational needs. This is strongly reflected in the way employers react to applicants with broad interests:

> *My diverse background has served me well. Though I was a physics and Russian studies major, potential employers in the field of computing are very interested in my unconventional background.*
>
> —*Ted Wallace, age 26*

Why would computing companies see value in a student's knowledge of Russian studies? Probably because the most rapid growth in demand for hardware and software in coming years is going to be in foreign markets. Russia, like China, is potentially one of the largest of these. Differences in language, culture, and markets are formidable, and a manager who is able to bridge these differences may contribute significant additional value to the company.

But there's more. Who is going to do better when faced in the future again and again with the need to master subject matter and skills that can't be foreseen precisely in advance? Will it be the person who "followed the dots" in taking courses and gaining experience in a single conventional specialty—perhaps the only specialty he could find that is suited well enough to his own particular preferences and talents to allow him to succeed? Or will it be the person who has already shown that he can excel in diverse and challenging areas of thought and work? Most likely the latter.

There's no premium on being scattered and shallow. The premium is on having shown the will and the means to master and excel in more than one endeavor, preferably endeavors that can be read as having some potential relevance to future job activities.

> When I am interviewing people right out of college, I look for them to have juggled many different balls and to have gotten good grades. I also want them to have a vision of where they are going so that they are entrepreneurial and don't need their hands held all the time.

—Sally Pipes, President, Pacific Research Institute

An entrepreneur is a person who can undertake almost any task needed to move the business ahead. He's a generalist rather than a specialist. If you have done a number of different kinds of things successfully, then you're more likely to be able to master a new activity without needing "your hand held all the time." This makes you more valuable not only because you can do more, but because you will need less training and supervision. You will be a self-starter who can finish a task without needing a lot of additional fuel.

The Foreign Dimension

The more you've done and been involved in, the more of an appealing candidate you'll be. I had lived and studied in Paris, been a member of the honors society and the chess club and membership chair of my sorority.

—*Abby Wittenberg, age 25*

Why did Abby's experience living in France make her a more appealing candidate? One reason is that as globalization proceeds and the world continues to "get smaller," the importance for companies of having people who can span borders and continents becomes greater.

Bilingualism—and better yet, biculturalism—are highly attractive attributes in a job candidate.

But it's unlikely that many of those companies that made offers to Abby did so because they had, or expected to have, a critical need for people who could be effective in a French-speaking environment. More likely, these employers saw Abby's accomplishment as a strong demonstration of—you guessed it—her adaptability. Others might have wilted in an unfamiliar setting, or had trouble communicating and getting things done. Abby—at least by her own account—didn't.

Every company has its own culture and jargon. At the beginning, these will be unfamiliar to you. If such a situation renders you timid and ineffectual, then your prospects for weaving yourself into the fabric of the organization will be poor. If Abby can adapt to France, then she is more likely to be able to adapt to Company X. She will be able to understand what her boss and coworkers want, and in turn to make herself understood and respected. She will avoid doing the things that would distract or antagonize individuals whose experiences and expectations are different from her own.

A student who had clearly been successful in adapting to an even more unfamiliar working environment, such as China or Egypt, might be accorded even more points for adaptability by interviewers. The less familiar another culture is, the more dramatically it differs from our own, the more you will stand out when you present yourself as one of the few who have mastered it.

> *The key to getting a job is how you distinguish yourself. When I was at Booz, Allen & Hamilton, I would see 5,000 résumés and we would ultimately extend offers to 200 of those.*
>
> —*Eric Zausner, former partner at Booz, Allen & Hamilton*

That gives you a four percent chance of getting hired. Such a small hiring rate is not at all unusual for top companies. Demonstrated ability to adapt to unusual situation distinguishes you from the other candidates. It catches the eye and pulls your résumé out of the pack.

When David Bruce was the American ambassador to France, he needed to hire a personal assistant. One applicant's résumé said she spoke seven languages. The job didn't require seven languages, but the qualification was so unusual that it made this résumé jump out of the stack. Guess who he hired?

Where Are All the Employers?

12

Before you start looking for employers, you need to learn about employers. This will help you align your preparation and the way you present yourself with the needs of appropriate employers. You can get part of the information you need from professors and other contacts who already have a perspective on employment in the fields that interest you.

> *It's important that you find a professor or someone in the industry who can give you perspective on the job market and a sense of the shape and future of the field in which you are interested.*

> —*Roy Levin, Director, Systems Research Center, Digital Equipment Corporation*

Ideally, this process should start early in your college years, so that you can use what you learn in seeking internships and in choosing courses and other activities. You won't want to rely solely on any one person's prognostications and advice, but a mentor's perspective will provide a base line against which to bounce your other observations and inquiries. Often, there are crucial differences between what is out there today and what you should expect to encounter tomorrow.

*When I was in college, everything was mainframes, big systems,
and one-off applications. Most students were thinking IBM. I was
very fortunate that my mentor turned my attention towards PCs
and networking. Otherwise I'd have been obsolete before I started.*

—*Henry, age 33*

Although universities have led in many areas of research, professors'
interests may evolve much less rapidly than the marketplace. Training you
for employment is not necessarily a major goal of your department. Your
professors' points of view need to be checked against what you hear in the
workplace, especially if your professors are not active in consulting or other
entrepreneurial or industry activity.

Course offerings in your department might not feature what you're going to
need for your first job, much less what you're going to need in the next five
years. Your choice of classes and your search for internships and jobs should
be guided by industry reality, rather than by the course catalogue and the
requirements of your major.

*A lot of computer science courses still focus on algorithmic
languages such as C++, but what you should be learning now is
Java. It's not a very difficult language, but why waste time learning
others that you aren't going to need?*

—*Milton, age 25*

Finding the Employers You Will Target

A few employers will come looking for you, or at least they will get as far as your placement office, where it's easy for you to make contact. You might even get some letters soliciting your interest in an employer, especially if you belong to an organization that focuses on a technical field such as electrical engineering. There may also be at least a few employers with which you already are in touch, or where you have a point of contact that you can readily activate.

Those possibilities may seem like they are already a lot to handle. In fact, you might easily book yourself solid with placement office interviews. But it's important to recognize just how tiny a fraction of the potential employers these few really are. There are over a million businesses in the United States. Add to that the thousands of governmental units and agencies, more thousands of nonprofit and nonbusiness employers, and an even longer list of possible international and foreign opportunities, some of which involve teaching. In total, there are far more employers, even in your own region or city, than you could ever manage to know about, much less evaluate and compare so as to make an informed choice between them.

> Your employment options are not limited to the jobs offered by recruiters who come to your campus or the jobs you see advertised in the newspaper.

If you're passive and simply process whatever possibilities come your way through your contacts and your scanning of ads and lists, then you are likely to miss some excellent opportunities. It's difficult for employers to find you, so it's worthwhile for you to make some effort to find them. The first problem you will encounter, however, is that they are all too easy to find. You can see masses of unfamiliar company names in industry publications and marketing materials.

> *Once you have a sense of your life goals or a list of skills you want to gain from your first job, get your résumé out to every firm out there that might help you achieve those goals. Get a directory of firms involved in the industries you're interested in and send résumés to all of them. From there, follow up with phone calls and get your foot in the door.*

—Beth, age 23

Since employers, like sites on the Internet, are just too numerous to scan or flip through, you will need to make your search efficient, rather than either random or exhaustive. There is a lot about employers that you have to see or hear for yourself. You can't find everything you need to know in a book or brochure. But at least there are data sources that are helpful in seeking the right employer, and that is seldom the case when you're seeking the right person.

Many students, knowing that their skills are of a very general nature, feel more comfortable seeking employment with companies that are likewise very broad in their scope of activity. They see no reasonable way to choose one highly specialized company or product category over another. In addition, they like the idea of working for an organization with which they feel more comfortable because its name is well known.

This can lead to tunnel vision, greatly limiting the range of choice. The student who is willing to go outside the ranks of large and well known employers can generate a larger number of more interesting choices.

Fooling around on the Internet, I ran into sites that really interested me, that I went back to again and again. A couple of them had employment info, but others didn't, so I just called them up. I started by telling them why I liked their sites. I got some really interesting interviews.

—Sally, age 22

The principle is far more general than that. Scratch together a list of products and services you really like, including the ones you use all the time without your even thinking consciously about how much you like them. Knowing something about a company and its products, feeling enthusiastic about them, are two big stepping stones towards a productive discussion about employment. You may not know whether you're headed towards marketing or towards service, but if you appreciate what a company delivers then you will be talking to the right people.

Faxing your résumé around to a ton of companies is the worst thing you can do. Concentrate on an industry and pick two or three companies within that industry. Then you can take the time to understand the industry and the specificities of the particular companies. You can go into an interview and say: "I know companies like yours are facing problems of this sort and I have come up with a way of solving that problem." You've got to be proactive in telling potential employers what you can bring to their organization.

—Tom Gardner, cofounder, The Motley Fool

Making Contact

It's easy to get a switchboard number for a company. If you don't know where its headquarters is located, you can search on the Internet. But once you call the number, what do you tell the person who answers? Sally had a straightforward approach that worked fine:

> *I would just say I was graduating in a few months, loved their products, and was interested in employment. Almost every time, the operator put me in touch with the right person right away.*

—*Sally, age 22*

Every successful enterprise is looking for good people. Even if a company is not growing, it has to replace employees who leave. The entry level is the most logical place to do most of this hiring, because the great majority of employers prefer to promote from within. Only very small companies, or those that are struggling financially are likely to tell you: "No, we're not hiring any college students."

Once you have the right person on the phone, preferably a decision maker or manager rather than an assistant who will merely relay your information up the line, you then need to give a very highly condensed and focused version of your résumé. In Sally's case, this was, for example: "I've had a few software courses and I also enjoy selling. Your site development products give me all kinds of good ideas! Can I make an appointment to come in next week and talk about a job for when I graduate in June?"

Most likely, the human resources person is going to want to see a résumé as soon as possible, but that won't stop Sally from trying to pin down an appointment right away. You want the hirer to have to make as few favorable decisions as possible between the first contact and the job offer. The last thing you want is to have to send a résumé, have the hirer forget the phone call, and then have to get the person's attention again to schedule an interview.

> *We receive tens of thousands of unsolicited résumés. About 10 percent of the people who send unsolicited résumés are granted an interview.*
>
> *—Andrea Beldecos, Director of College Recruiting, J.P. Morgan & Co.*

Ten percent is a fairly small chance of success, but it's not much trouble to send a résumé, so the effort may seem justified. However, the great majority of the ten percent who got interviewed probably did a lot more than use the mail. They most likely called to follow up, possibly with other people in the organization.

In general, "send your résumé" is a way to get you off the phone. "We can't find your résumé" is a way to put you off again. You can win this battle of wits by making an unexpected move. Try saying, "I'm going to be down near you on Wednesday afternoon. Can I come in around four o'clock?" Or, "These résumés keep getting lost; they all look alike. Can I come down and hand deliver it and at least shake hands with you? How about tomorrow morning at 10?"

> *We don't hire a lot of undergraduates. One way of differentiating yourself is getting in the door to see someone. We get thousands of*

résumés, but the ones with a note by someone from the company attached are the ones that get a second glance.

—*Kiko Washington, VP of Human Resources, HBO*

In many companies, even small ones, hiring is not centralized. Even if the marketing department and the development department each comprise only a few people, they may hire separately. Thus, at the very outset you may be asked which division or function you're interested in. Don't be afraid to ask for a run down of the possibilities, because every company is organized somewhat differently from the others, and the organization structure is prone to change. The more you know about the company, the more possibilities you can unearth.

If more than one division appeals to you, pick the first one that comes to mind or say something like, "Why don't we try marketing first." If the first choice doesn't lead to an interview, you should call back and ask for the next one, continuing until all the possibilities of interest to you have been exhausted. No one person is in a position to turn you down on behalf of the entire organization. If you get nowhere at one location, try another.

Even in the most centralized company, the fact that there's one office charged with the mission of handling all college recruitment actually means very little. If a local or functional manager wants to have you considered for a job, the central recruitment office will say, "Yes, ma'am." So, go after the sales, the service or the lab manager, each of whom has more than enough authority to get you hired. You can accomplish more with the decision makers than with the functionaries, unless the job you want is as a human resources professional.

You've got to be very aggressive on the search side of the recruiting process, especially if you're not quite sure what you want to do. It's amazing how many interviews you can get if you put your mind to it.

—*Mark Leferman, age 24*

If you set your mind to it, commit the necessary time and effort, and are willing and able to adapt and learn from experience, then you can get the interviews you want.

Digging for Additional Possibilities

A great many organizations that are good prospective employers will have names and even products that initially are unfamiliar to you. So, how do you find them?

I wanted to stay in Wisconsin, if possible. So, I riffled through copies of local and regional newspapers and magazines to see what companies had been making news in the state. If the news looked appealing, I got the phone number and called.

—*Annette, age 22*

A news story, especially if it's a fairly recent one, most often will tell you something that the company is happy about and wants the world to know and talk about. It may be about a big contract, a new product, or the appointment of a new executive. The origin of most of these stories is a news release issued by the company or its public relations firm.

Almost all states and many cities also have a Department of Trade and Industry, Chamber of Commerce, or a similar official organization whose aim is to promote the expansion of business there. These organizations compile lists and further information about companies that are coming into or expanding in their territory.

> *I called and said "The Department of Trade told me you're expanding your customer service center here and will add 50 new people. Who is handling the recruitment for customer service positions?"*
>
> —*Annette, age 22*

The expansion is merely the peg on which Annette hung her first lines of dialogue. Maybe there will be no new desks to fill for another 18 months, but that doesn't really matter. Referring to the expansion gave Annette a dollop of additional credibility. It's better than "Are you hiring now?"

There are a large number of magazines and newspapers that report business news on a national basis. The magazines are easy to find by sweeping through the library, or by looking at the titles in an index of periodicals. The magazines often approach companies from an intriguing or controversial angle. *Forbes*, for example, regularly carries a large number of brief articles about companies, many of which have an unfavorable slant.

> *His name was in the article, so I called up and told his secretary that I wanted to talk to him about errors in the* Forbes *story. When I got him, I told him how unfair I thought the article was. I must have hit him on a day when he felt the whole world was against him. He was very happy to interview me.*
>
> —*Lester, age 24*

Why would you want to work for a company that has attracted unfavorable publicity? Think about it this way: there are probably some people that just plain don't like you, so give executives and companies the benefit of the same doubt. You have a less favorable side, and so do they. You won't choose an employer primarily on the basis of publicity, whether it's favorable or unfavorable. But any company where you can readily persuade an executive to give you an interview is well worth pursuing. When do you think it's easier to get an interview at Microsoft: When they are on top of the world, or when they are feeling embattled and persecuted?

The Internet as a Resource

Smaller and newer companies are most easily sought out on the Internet.

> *Our clients are small, but fast-growing startup companies. The companies tend not to have the budget for visists to colleges and universities, and so they go through the Internet to save time and money.*

—*Rachel Bell, cofounder, JobDirect.com*

If you're interested in a company, you should always search for and visit its Internet site. The site will provide information about the company and how to make contact. Often there are descriptions of available jobs and an opportunity to apply for them. This is the most direct and the quickest and easiest way of taking an initial look at what a company has to offer.

The Internet also offers an increasing number of broader gauged employment-oriented sites where hiring companies and job-seeking students can get in contact. Some of the sites are established by individual companies, but are open for use by unaffiliated companies. Other sites, such as JobDirect.com, are hosted by independent enterprises whose business is recruiting.

As use of the Internet expands, such sites will become more numerous, more populated with companies and students, and more functional. Before deciding which site or sites to use, check out the number of relevant companies and the number of job descriptions or requests included at each site you're interested in. Review the dates to ensure that what you're seeing is not obsolete.

> If you neglect the Internet, you're behind the crowd. A remarkable number of students already are using this medium, and they are not all engineering and technical students by any means.

Throughout 1997, we had résumés from over 100,000 students on our site. Many of the employers on the site have jobs for nontechnical students.

—*Rachel Bell, cofounder, JobDirect.com*

HR managers are aware that students and other employers are moving onto the Internet. Hence, many of them put an emphasis on their Internet recruitment efforts that is more consistent with their hopes for the future than with their accomplishments to date.

Can you tell me how to get students to send me their résumés on the Internet? They don't come to our site, and I don't know which other sites we should use to bring them in. So far, it looks like we're not performing.

—Human resources manager, consumer service industry

Such managers will gladly give attention to students who come to their own corporate site. They are also increasingly likely to sign up with other recruitment sites.

The first thing you can do at an employment site is to read up on employers and look at the positions they are offering. For some reason, in this electronic medium, employers are often more communicative about qualities they are looking for in applicants than is the case in printed recruitment brochures. The Internet information can be more up to date, and it's also more results oriented, if only because the company can read its success at snagging applications in real time.

Some employment sites also offer you assistance in preparing a résumé. This not only helps you put the résumé in an appropriate format, but also outlines the information that should be included and provides writing tips. Once your résumé is available in this form, it will be easy to update and improve, and can generally by moved onto other sites or transmitted via e-mail.

Finally, you can apply for jobs on the Internet by completing application forms and e-mailing your résumé and any other information you want to include. This is quite different from sending a blind résumé through the mail, because the company has solicited your interest through its decision to advertise at the site. Its failure to respond could result in a complaint to the organization hosting the site, so your chance of establishing contact through this channel should be more favorable.

Often, information obtained on the Internet or even a job application completed there can provide a starting point. Then you can and should follow up, saying something like: "I sent in my application online, but I am not sure it got through. Who handles the online applications?" This is more likely to get you some attention than "I mailed in my résumé and I haven't heard anything yet."

> With the mail, it amounts to "Don't call us, we'll call you." Or, "Send another one." The Internet volume is lower, and they're more concerned about it. It's easier to get attention.

—*Janet, age 22*

How Can You Make Yourself Irresistible to Employers?

You don't have to be irresistible to get a first interview. The interview represents only a small commitment of effort on the part of the hiring organization, and lots of people who get interviewed are not extraordinary. Nevertheless, unless the interview is arranged through your college placement office, to get it you're going to have to soar like a sky rocket from a heap of résumés that will get little if any attention. In making that happen, your initiative in making personal contact with the employer will be more important than anything included in your résumé.

It's at the interview stage that you need to be irresistible. It's here that employers are most keen to avoid mistakes: That's why there are normally two or three rounds of interviews, each one involving two or more company representatives. To pass this peculiar, multiround "oral exam," you need to be well prepared, proactive, and focused. Your chances of just winging it and making things up as you go along might seem reasonably good if there were only one interview. But most employers are careful. To get through six or ten interviewers and finally get a job offer, you need to have a well thought out and practiced set of messages to communicate.

Job hunting, preparing to interview, and interviewing are hard work. There are only so many hours in the day. Lightening your course load during the semester in which you plan to do a lot of interviewing is a good option to consider.

> *During recruiting season, I recommend taking one less class. You will need the extra time to do research on the companies with which you're seeking employment, complete applications, interview on campus and travel to interviews onsite.*

—*Jason Martinez, age 25*

> It's not enough to allocate time and effort to the recruiting process. You have also got to be organized. Start early so that you maximize your possibilities and get the highest possible return on your effort.

> *I wish I had taken more time to keep abreast of the variety of employment opportunities available to me, and their deadlines. I didn't realize that one of the top firms interviewed really early and I completely missed the opportunity to take a job at that firm.*

—*J. B. Mantz, age 25*

Preparing for Interviews

You don't always prepare for class, and you might not always prepare for interviews. The problem is that one class session won't affect your grade much, while one interview is easily enough to lose you an employment opportunity. And you will have a fairly small number of such opportunities in your senior year. Don't waste any.

Some of your interview preparations will be applicable to all or many employers, while some will relate to one specific employer. One important component of your general preparation relates to your résumé: You need to be ready to answer challenging questions about each item listed there.

> The biggest mistake students make today is to write up an absolutely fabulous résumé that they can't defend. Anything on a student's resume is fair game and the student has got to be prepared to answer questions about it.
>
> —Jim Gwinn, Director of Global Staffing, American Cyanamid Company

Focus first on the points in your résumé that are most likely to catch an interviewer's attention. These will typically include your work experience, any leadership positions you have held, and your studies.

> I spent over three years on my college education before my interviews. I spend the equivalent of two full weeks preparing for my interviews. In terms of getting job offers, seems like the two weeks were at least as important as the three years.
>
> —Arnold, age 22

Put yourself (or a roommate or friend) in the interviewer's position, and draft a rough list of the most obvious questions. "Tell me about your internship with Hewlett Packard." Or, "How did you get such a high GPA?"

(Alternatively, if it's not so high, "Which courses didn't you do well in?") "What did you accomplish as editor of the paper?" "How did you get chosen as captain of the soccer team, and how did you handle the challenges of the job?" Then, after the first mock interview, expand and refine the list. Repeat this process several times. Make sure you have better answers the next time than you had the last time—every time.

But before you work on your answers, get clear on what makes an answer effective. Your answers need to be responsive, consistent, brief, clear, interesting, and defensible. Most of all, they need to present you as a person whom an employer should want to hire. You shouldn't be vague or evasive, and you shouldn't say anything that you might have to shade or retract later. Each answer should be designed to lead the conversation in a positive direction, one that is advantageous to you and will highlight your strengths and selling points.

Work out answers that fit the bill. Dash them out on your computer. Try them in your practice sessions. Get comfortable enough with them so that you're not groping for exact words, but are expressing yourself freely, fluently, and convincingly. You can't afford the luxury of being either boring or tongue-tied.

Your campus placement office may offer workshops or other resources to help you prepare for interviews. It may even offer a videotaping service that lets you record one of your mock interviews. Take advantage of these resources. Seeing a tape of yourself in an interviewing situation can be highly illuminating. You may realize that you have a few verbal and nonverbal habits that you need to break before your real interviews. Verbal problems include speaking too rapidly, rambling, mumbling, using too many slang terms, and using verbal fillers that make you sound inarticulate ("um," "like," "ya know?"). Nonverbal problems include fidgeting, slouching, failing to maintain reasonable eye contact with your interviewer, or crossing your arms across your chest (this makes you seem frightened and defensive).

Apart from the questions that any interviewer might reasonably be expected to ask on the basis of your résumé and other credentials, there's another set of questions that you also need to ask and answer. These are the questions that interviewers simply tend to ask—year after year. You will hear about them from friends who were interviewed the previous year, and you will remember them from interviews you have had for internships or other work. These are questions like: "Tell me about the greatest challenge you have faced, and how you responded to it." Or, "Tell me about the biggest failure or disappointment you had, and why it happened."

When you have your list of these questions down, work on a set of answers with minimum overlap or duplication. Again, aim to sell yourself as an employee by showcasing, explicitly or most likely implicitly, the qualities that employers are most eager to find. These qualities include adaptability, interpersonal skills of collaboration and leadership, insight, and most of all, successful performance in situations that resemble the work situation as closely as possible.

How can you put your best profile forward without boasting? How can you graciously admit some small weaknesses and mistakes while focusing on your ability to learn and to overcome difficulties? Those are some of the dilemmas you need to resolve before the first interview. The way to do so is by practice interviewing with friends, particularly some who have already had substantial interview experience.

Senior year, my friends and I sat around the room and bounced interview questions off of each other. The practice was helpful and it put us into the interviewing mindset.

—Jason Martinez, age 25

It's even better if you can do your mock interviewing with friends who have already completed the recruitment process.

Set up mock interviews in which friends who have recently graduated fire questions at you. If you do that, you'll be much better prepared and feel much more confident when you go for your actual interviews.

—Thomas, age 29

You need also to leave time to prepare for interviews with specific companies. Make phone calls to get more company data than is supplied through the placement office. In particular, get everything that the shareholder relations office of the company is able to send you. At a minimum, you need the company's annual financial report and its mission and vision statement. Use Internet search engines to dig up even more.

Successful candidates have done good research. They have asked people about our product and can answer the question: 'What makes our product a great product?'

—Jim Gwinn, Director of Global Staffing, American Cyanamid Company

What you know about a company shows your interest in and enthusiasm for that company. It enables you to avoid putting your foot in your mouth, and it helps you direct the course of the conversation by commenting on and asking questions about aspects of what the company is doing.

> *When I did recruiting of college graduates at Prudential, I was impressed when candidates had a sense of capital markets and interest rate movements. To be successful, candidates have got to learn about the industry and the style of the firm. Read the paper, visit the career center library and speak to as many people who work at the firm as you can.*
>
> *—John Rigos, cofounder of Cductive.com*

How Do You Impress an Interviewer?

A number of attributes and accomplishments that can make you more attractive to employers have been mentioned in prior chapters. These include your GPA, your internships and other work experience, and any other evidence you can give that shows your versatility and effectiveness. None of these things, or even all of them together, can make you irresistible to an employer.

> There's only one quality that can make you irresistible: your evident enthusiasm for the employer and the job.

If you have it, this enthusiasm will show in your tone of voice, your facial expression, the questions you ask, and the answers you give. If you don't have it, your interview can at best be a lukewarm success, leaving crucial doubts in the interviewer's mind. What are you really after? Would you take the job if offered? How long would you stay?

> *It's important to be upbeat and positive during interviews. Interviewers like to see confidence and congeniality. It's also essential that you make it appear that you have a genuine interest in the job.*
>
> —John, age 24

Why is enthusiasm so important in getting employers to want you? There are several reasons. One is that unrequited love is a pretty unpleasant experience. No interviewer wants to go to bat for you, get the approval to make you an offer—and then have you turn the offer down. His success comes from getting the right people to sign on, not in merely making offers.

At a more fundamental level, you have probably noticed that almost all the people you really like are people who also like and appreciate you. If a person is doubtful, neutral, skeptical, or hesitant about you, then you're not likely to welcome him into your inner circle and spend time with him. It's the same for any group, or for an organization. If you like them, this implies shared values and purposes, compatibility, and a natural desire to be together.

In addition, if you're enthusiastic about the company and job, then you're far more likely to keep focused on your work and on your longer term future in the company. You won't be looking around from day one, waiting for someone to come rushing up to you with a better offer. Nor will you be demoralizing your fellow workers by telling them what is wrong with the company or how sorry you are to be with them.

Of course, enthusiasm is impressive only if sincere:

> *Be sincere in the interview. I once interviewed someone who was so overly enthusiastic that she seemed like a cheerleader. Her attempts to impress me backfired.*

> —Maritza Solari, Director of Medical Staff Services, California Pacific Medical Center

Demonstrating Enthusiasm

Enthusiasm is not just a set of gestures, it also has to be reflected in your actions. Coming a little early, appropriately dressed, and with copies of the company's documents and of your own in hand is at least a start. Signing up for an interview, then showing up with a big smile and absolutely no knowledge about the company doesn't show enthusiasm. The earlier you start making contact and the more time you spend finding out about and interacting with the company, the more your enthusiasm at the interview will be recognized as both genuine and as rooted in facts and understanding rather than myth or dreams.

> *I wish I had known more about the finance industry before my interviews. Interviewers ask why you are interested in their industry and firm, and you have got to have a good answer.*

> —Mark Leferman, age 24

In the traditional, high-volume, senior-year interviewing process, with one interview coming right after another and in the midst of classes and papers, it's easy to get dinged for lack of enthusiasm or commitment. But there's more to it than that. Think about the recruiter who has just gone through two or three days in which she is seeing a new student every half hour or hour. At the end of that time, she has to decide which five or six out of twenty students are going to be invited back for the next round of interviews.

Well, luckily she has a list and the résumé book. Otherwise, she would already have forgotten more than half of them. (You would probably have forgotten them, too.) Then she tries to remember the interviews. She has some notes, and she may have marked some boxes on a form. Not much to go on. But, which interviews can she actually remember in any relevant way?

> *Making an impact is extremely important during the interview. We don't want a raving nut, but we want someone who leaves an impression on the interviewer.*
>
> —*Jim Gwinn, Director of Global Staffing, American Cyanamid Company*

Perhaps a few people will be remembered for something especially idiotic or embarrassing that they said or did. But you can't expect to be a winner in this round merely by avoiding disaster. Those who have already been forgotten have probably been forgotten forever. They will be left off the list for the next round.

You will be among the few that the interviewer remembers favorably if you have engaged her. Because the discussion wasn't merely perfunctory, but became personally expressive, of her as well as of you. That can happen only if your enthusiasm was sufficient to arouse her own engagement. How do you do this?

I wanted the job very badly. So, I went to their own library—where else would I find more information about their organization? Turned out I was the only candidate who had gotten the inside scoop. They hired me.

—Rick, age 57

The supposed primary subject of any job interview is you, rather than the company, the interviewer, or the job. That is because the other elements of the situation are all constant: It's the students who differ, and the interviewer's task is to reveal and sort out these differences. The hitch is right there. Although you may find yourself fascinating, you are not a very stimulating centerpiece for someone who is spending at least a few days talking to 19 other "you's," each of whom is equally interested in himself. Bring the company and the interviewer into the spotlight with you.

The main things interviewers are looking for during the interview are energy and enthusiasm, the ability to think on one's feet, and a good personality.

—Steve Bowsher, E*Trade Group

If you relate well to the interviewer, she will perceive you as having a good personality. It's up to you to turn the interview from a monologue punctuated by interrogation into an interesting conversation. You do this by drawing on the interviewer's experiences and interests, by finding common ground on which you can draw together. Say little about anything that is not worth remembering.

In order for the interview to be a conversation, you have to be responsive so that the interviewer can also feel free to be responsive. You have to pick up on nuances and clues such as facial expression and the speed with which the interviewer responds to what you say.

> *I thought I had a great interview. I was articulate, coherent, and persuasive—I thought. The interviewer kept a polite poker face throughout and he didn't even have to say very much. I was amazed when I wasn't invited back.*
>
> *—Tracy, age 22*

If the interviewer is not saying much, then what is he thinking about? Is it the undone work piling up on his desk at the office while he wastes his time listening to you spout off? Has he been daydreaming? To avoid boring your interviewer or giving his mind time to wander, keep you answers to all questions concise. As you may have learned while you sat in classes or when you gave a talk to a class or another group, the human attention span is very limited.

> *Whether your internship is paid or unpaid, for credit or not for credit is unimportant. What matters is that you can talk about what you did and what you learned during your internship in a concise manner.*
>
> *—Andrew Ackerman, age 26*

One way to keep your interviewer engaged is to end some of your answers with questions about the company. To do it every time would be too mechanical, so sprinkle your questions throughout the interview. If the interviewer doesn't seem to like it, then stop. But this is one way of relieving the interviewer of the need to constantly think up a new topic or angle of attack, and to move your meeting towards dialogue. Try this technique when you do practice interviews with friends.

If there's a slight gap or uncomfortable pause in the conversation, have questions ready. Not dumb and impersonal questions about the company, but questions that elicit personal insight. "How did *you* pick this company over your other job offers?" "What projects are you working on now?" "Are you planning to go back for more education?" You want to recast the interviewer's role from that of judge to that of mentor and advisor. If he's spending time trying to help you or to sell you on the company rather than trying to poke holes in your résumé, then he's already assuming that you're going to get an offer.

> *Obviously, not every interview was going to lead to a job! But I looked at each interview as an opportunity to add to my Filofax one more person who could be of help to me later. I intend to keep in touch with most of these people, and our conversations identified mutual interests.*
>
> —*Kent, age 22*

The interviewer's engagement with you in the interview will help him remember you and make your interview stand out. But you must also communicate things that he will retain as especially demonstrative of why you should be hired. When you tell about a special accomplishment, or say something about the company and why you want to work there, be ready to express yourself with words that will be retained. You need at least a few images or words that are vivid and compelling. Humor can be a great help.

What Is the Interviewer Looking For?

> Directionally, if not literally, the interviewer's decision for or against you is very much like a decision as to whether he wants you working right beside him. If you are boring or inarticulate, you will be off the list. If you are brief, responsive, clear, and capable of being funny, then you are a person he would like to have around.

The interviewer doesn't ask questions in order to learn the factual answer, to be polite, or to gratify her curiosity, but rather in order to evaluate qualities you have that will determine your success in the job. Each company instructs its interviewers to focus on those qualities that are thought to be the most predictive of the value you will have when employed by the company. The list of qualities varies somewhat from company to company. Here is a typical example:

> *We look to see evidence of five core competencies during the interview process: analytical skills, communications skills, teamwork and leadership skills, results orientation and knowledge of the industry. We want people who will fit with our core values of excellence, respect, and meritocracy. Beyond the basic skills, we are looking for candidates who are confident risk takers and are willing to think outside of the box and take initiative.*

> —*Andrea Beldecos, Director of College Recruiting, J.P. Morgan*

Now, imagine that each interviewer has a sheet in front of her, based on Andrea's statement. The first row is for analytical skills, the second for communications skills, and the last one is for initiative. She's going to put pluses on these lines during the interview if you convince her that you have these qualities. She will put minuses if you give the impression that you lack the qualities.

If you fail to see a piece of paper or notebook at the interviewer's fingertips, don't imagine for a minute that you've escaped this evaluative process. She's trying to keep all these ratings in her head, or to combine and balance them informally to come up with an overall evaluation. One way or the other, she's accountable for rating you on each of these scales.

So, everything you say, whether it's modest or exaggerated, whether it's fascinating or boring, is going to get boiled down to some pluses and minuses—just as everything you do in all your classes gets boiled down to a grade and then a GPA. When the interviewer asks you an unexpected question, it may be hard on the spur of the moment and without practice to come up with an answer that gives you plenty of pluses and no minuses. When you're asked a question that is pretty close to one you should have expected, then your answer should be closer to the bullseye. In either case, preparation and practice will pay off.

Showing You Have Initiative

In your preparation, you need to think about what examples and lines of argument you can use to get the obvious pluses. Let's take initiative as an example of an area in which you want plusses. Come up with two or three events or successes of the kind that will establish that you're a person of conspicuous initiative. And don't go back to the time you stood on top of two chairs to get the jam at age four. Anything before college won't count.

I want to hire people who have proven in college that they are problem solvers, that they can overcome difficulties. An example? When I was in college, I wanted to learn computer science, but most of the courses in that field were supposedly open only to graduate students. Yet I wangled my way into each of them. That was problem solving!

—*Stephen Billard, director of software development, Pacific Development Labs*

You may need to reinterpret, stretch, and embroider. You may need to check that your version of each story is understandable, interesting, and likely to be interpreted so as to credit you with the pluses that you need. But one way or the other, you must figure out how to come across as imbued with initiative. This is the quality that enables you to do what could not be achieved by purely routine means. Initiative permits you to gain your goal in an unexpected way, eluding the obvious obstacles.

Someone who worked at Nickelodeon came to speak on campus. I went up to him after the speech to ask about internship opportunities. He told me to write him a letter, which I did. I then met with him for an informational interview and he set me up with an interview for an internship. I ended up working at Nickelodeon for the summer. A little bit of initiative can get you a long way.

—*Aaron Katz, age 25*

Interviewers, being canny characters, are not likely to come right out and say: "Please tell me a time that you showed initiative." But you can expect that they will ask you something, or give you an opportunity to say something about your internships. And if you're well prepared, you will seize on that question to tell how you got the internship or succeeded brilliantly in the internship—in a way that required initiative.

Highlighting Your Teamwork and Leadership Skills

Now turn to two other qualities that were on the list, teamwork and leadership. Almost any job except taxi driving calls for those qualities. How do you assure yourself of a plus on that line?

> *We need team players, not prima donnas. You can prove you're a team player by your success working in a team on a class project, or in a lab group, or on a sports team.*
>
> —Stephen Billard, Director of Software Development, Pacific Development Labs

Unless you're applying for a solo role at the Metropolitan Opera, you better not be a prima donna. But this quote confirms that you can earn your team player status without having actually to play on a (sports) team. However, it may be a little harder to do it that way. A recruiter is more likely to ask, "Did you play on any teams?" than to ask, "Did you have any successful experiences in working as a member of a group?" The second question seems vague, and it almost invites you to scratch your head and come up with something or other, probably weak.

So, if you can't tell a stirring story about your generous and helpful teamwork on the gridiron, then you will need to apply some of your preparation time to thinking about what it is you have done that can get you that essential plus for teamwork. Maybe it was a major class project. Maybe it was as a manager or officer of a student organization. Maybe it was something you did in your dormitory or sorority. It would be handy to have a couple of incidents at hand, not just one.

> *In most of my interviews, I told how I had gotten friends together to put a stop to loud and disturbing parties in our dorm. I could see this went over very effectively every time.*

—Sharon, age 22

Each story has to be brief and focused: a success story with a pivot point that is your contribution to the group. Once you have selected one or two of these incidents and cut and shaped them for easy and pointed retelling, you will then come up with notions of how to fit them into the interview. This is the hard part. You can't just drag a good story in by its ear, as in "Did I tell you the one about how . . . ?" The story has to find a natural and logical place in the probable flow of dialogue at the interview.

For instance, you may have a great story showing how you helped raise the money to keep your sorority house from being foreclosed by the bank. But where is that story going to fit into the interview? Perhaps it can be presented as the answer to a question about challenges you have faced, or about your most gratifying accomplishments, or about out-of-class learnings in college. (Of course, if you're really lucky, there might be a point-blank question about teamwork.) For each of these scenarios, you will need a slightly different slant, to be thought through in advance. Overall, your preparation must give you a reasonable range of choice as to how to use your anecdotes.

Showing Off Your Communications Skills

Communications skills are another one of those important qualities most employers seek. The interview itself is likely to be seen as a test of how strong you are in this area.

> *The ability to communicate effectively will be essential to your success in whatever job you take after graduation. Use your college years to hone your communications skills.*
>
> *—Ted Wallace, age 25*

> *Communications skills are rarely taught in college but they are essential to success in business. I would advise college students to take communications classes and to hone their communications skills any other way they can, such as extracurriculars or job experience.*
>
> *—Ann Winblad, venture capitalist*

In most but not all cases, only your oral communications skills, which are the skills most essential in the majority of job situations, will actually be evaluated during the hiring process. In some fields, depending on what you have written, you may gain by bringing your written work to the interview.

> *Be sure to get internships that offer tangible skills that you can show off later—when you're looking for your first full-time job. For example, when working for my college newspaper, I catalogued all of my stories, keeping each one. When working in an internship for Xerox, I kept 100 copies of a corporate newsletter that I founded, coordinated, and developed. While working for the Los Angeles*

Clippers, I kept my collection of press releases, feature stories, and interview scripts. Later, when I went to my first real job interview, I was able to present all of these materials. The potential employer was impressed. Not only did I have an extensive background, but I had these tangible materials that he could really sink his teeth into. Even though I was monetarily compensated at only one of the five internships I had, I walked out of all of them with something very, very valuable.

—Greg Heilmann, age 24

Given that, like most other students, you're probably not going to be bringing term papers or other writing samples to your interviews, we can expect that your communications skills will be judged almost solely by what you say in the interview. But judged how? Is a recruiter going to ask you to express complex and profound thoughts in simple and compelling language? Will you be required to argue against Kant's categorical imperative, or in favor of the moral rights of smokers?

Not likely. It's much simpler than that. If you're scattered, slow, repetitive, and unconvincing during the interview, then you will be marked down for poor communication skills. If you're animated and interesting, if you easily hold the listener's attention while staying on the subject, then your communications skills will be graded appreciatively. So learn how to hold an audience of one while getting your points across.

Some employers will require you to face a larger audience.

Once people have made it through an initial screen with me, I invite them down to the lab to make a one-hour presentation followed by a 30-minute Q&A session to all of the employees in the meeting room. That's how I test a candidate's ability to communicate effectively.

—Brian Reid, Director of Network Systems Lab, Digital Equipment Corporation

Everything you say in an interview or a meeting has to serve a purpose. The overarching purpose is to get the job by strongly demonstrating all of the qualities the recruiter is looking for. Each statement aims at this purpose by giving you one or more pluses on the recruiter's mental or paperwork check list. It's up to you to prepare so that what you have to say is natural, engaging, and goal directed.

What Happens After the Interview?

Is a person going to be irresistible to an employer if, after the interview, he goes home and waits for the phone to ring? Well, that is certainly what most students do, and it doesn't seem to render them irresistible. There's a better way.

Immediately after each interview, I dropped a very brief note to the interviewer, picking up on our conversation, thanking him, and reaffirming my strong interest. Often I would leave voice mails, or call to thank them, and maybe ask an additional question. I think it made a difference.

—Jeremy, age 22

An interviewer sees lots of job seekers. Most of them, he realistically has no expectation of ever seeing again. He feels no connection with them, and little responsibility towards them. But when Jeremy resumes contact with an interviewer and thus steps out from the crowd, he has chosen this way to affirm his interest and determination. After hearing from him, the interviewer is likely to expect that if Jeremy doesn't make the next cut or doesn't get an offer, then he's likely to be back on the phone, asking why and asking what more he can do. That doesn't sound like much fun. The recruiter would rather have Jeremy calling to thank him. He might even do something to facilitate such an outcome. This gives him a gentle nudge in the right direction.

In fact, of course, Jeremy didn't get offers from every one of the companies he interviewed with. In some cases he failed to get past the first round. Every time this happened, he called each interviewer to ask what he was lacking, what could have made his case stronger. You can not expect that every time you ask those questions you will get an honest answer, much less a useful answer, but the questions is still worth asking.

> Every interview is a potential "keeper," a contact that can have value to you in the future. Some will even tell you: "I wanted them to make you an offer, but they got it wrong." It's worth finding these people. Sometimes you will be surprised at who they are.

Five years after I graduated, I ran into a guy at the airport. He remembered having interviewed me for my first job. "I sort of thought you might call me." Obviously, I missed an opportunity there.

—*Miguel, age 29*

Are the People Who Can Do the Job Best the Ones Who Get Hired?

Hiring processes are notoriously unreliable. Of those who join an organization at any level, a majority may be gone within a few years. If you're a reflective person, these facts might lead you to fear that after you have been offered and have accepted a job, you won't be able to perform adequately, thus setting yourself up either for failure or for a modest level of performance. If you can not trust the employer to determine how well you will perform, then how can you possibly make your own independent evaluation of your chances for success on the job?

This is an instance where what you saw in applying to college is again relevant. Many thousands of people who would do well at Harvard are denied admission because other candidates preferred by Harvard are available. The few people who fail at Harvard don't do so because they are not smart enough, or were poorly prepared. Similarly, very few of those who fail in their jobs do so because they lacked intelligence or technical knowledge. Most fail because they don't have the core skills and patterns of behavior that were identified in chapter 11.

We have seen in this chapter, however, that the capabilities that employers typically aim to evaluate in interviews (for instance, teamwork and initiative) are quite different from the ones discussed in chapter 11—the ones that seem to be most closely associated with success on the job (for instance, doing what the boss wants done). There are reasons for this divergence. What interviewer would have the nerve to try to evaluate whether you were going to do what the boss wanted? And even if he were game to try, how would he go about it? So, he aims instead to measure something that is thought to be both more observable and more universally admired, such as teamwork.

The differences between what a recruiter wants to see and what a boss wants to get are significant. The fact is that the people who are most desired by recruiters are not necessarily the ones who will perform best on the job.

> *We used to keep track of the people who got multiple offers, the ones we had to fight to get. The ones we hired didn't perform better than average, as far as we could make out. They were just people who interviewed well, I guess.*

—Andrew, age 34

What you do in college needs to prepare you to succeed in getting job offers. It also needs to prepare you to be successful on the job. There is some overlap between the two sets of requirements. However, each includes some items that are less relevant to the other, but that you must nonetheless satisfy.

Now That You Have the Job, What Will You Do with It?

Basically, what you have to do with your first job is to succeed in it. Even if the job is not what you expected, even if someone lied to you, even if you discover you have other, stronger interests, nevertheless, you have to perform excellently and achieve a clear success. The grass on the other side of the fence is always greener. But the only way to get to that greener grass is step by step.

Every new hire makes his own way in his first job experience. It's up to you to make this first experience a positive one, no matter what contradictions or constraints you encounter, and no matter how fervently you would prefer to be somewhere else.

> *Some people think, "It's just my first job, I can change course any time." That's a myth. My friends who aren't happy with their jobs are having trouble switching jobs now. You've got to take the time to think about what you really want to do before you take your first job.*
>
> *—Michael Bernstein, age 23*

It's not likely to be easy to change jobs quickly, unless you have another employer who wants you badly waiting in the background, so that you can switch jobs fast enough to avoid putting the first job on your résumé. You will be expected to account on your résumé for all your time starting in the fall following graduation, and an early job change shown on the résumé will be a distinct disadvantage. Furthermore, if your first employer learns that you're looking for another job, he may well retaliate—for instance, by firing you. There's no law against it. Hence, a discrete approach—and, consequently, a less rapid and urgent approach—to changing jobs is likely to be the only safe one. The same is true if you want to change bosses within your company. If your current boss figures out that you're leaving him because you didn't like or respect him, then he will probably prefer that you go as far away as possible to continue your career, so that you don't have the opportunity to broadcast your disrespect for him throughout the organization.

Performing Successfully

There is no machine or computer program that will be used to calculate how successfully you're doing the job. Even if your job is washing dishes, you are very unlikely to be rated by a mechanical and objective count of dishes washed vs. broken or dirty dishes. Most likely your job will be far too diffuse and complicated to make such an evaluation feasible, much less probable.

A single person will determine how well you have performed. Your boss will do this, almost singlehandedly. You're successful if, and only if, your boss says that you are. In fact, there will most likely be a formal evaluation process in which he is the key player.

We were supposed to be reviewed at least once a year, but it took them longer. I was staggered when my boss rated me in the "average" category. I thought I had been getting lots of encouragement and positive feedback all along.

—*Gregory, age 24*

Feedback from your boss is the key to performing more than satisfactorily. It's easier and more pleasant for the boss to maintain a pleasant facade than for him to carp and criticize constantly. His criticisms and suggestions may be obscured by a nonconfrontational style, so that they become almost subliminal. But Greg had many opportunities to ask. For instance, he might have asked: "I want to do a strong, above-average job. Did I accomplish that on this last assignment?"

To achieve success in the eyes of your boss, you need to be able to figure out what the boss wants from you, and then to deliver it. If you're unable or unwilling to do so, you will most likely be punished rather than rewarded, even if what you chose to do made more sense and had greater value (at least in your opinion) than what the boss had in mind. To know what you need to do to succeed, you need to figure out what the boss really wants and ask questions that will help reveal how he's going to judge what you do.

When it comes to any promotion or change of assignment you may be seeking within your company, your boss will surely be a major decision maker. If you leave the company, future employers may not talk to your old boss about you, but they will have other evidence as to how you have performed. Promotions and raises show that your work was appreciated. This is the kind of concrete proof of your value you want. But promotions and raises aren't automatic. In fact, you may get another, unwanted kind of assessment of your value: You may get fired.

I had read stories about pink slips, of course. I was shocked— speechless—when my boss called me in after three months and told me that this wasn't working out and that today would be my last day. I couldn't have been any more surprised and horrified if the doctor had said I had incurable cancer. I never failed before.

—Will, age 23

You may feel that you were fired because your boss didn't like you. You may be told that it happened because of a reorganization or downsizing. In any event, if you leave a job without having first gotten another one, then most people will assume that you were fired. This can make you a much less attractive hiring prospect. It's no longer a question of, "Why do you want to leave your present job?" The question now becomes, "What did you do wrong?" You can claim that you quit or that you left by mutual agreement, but these claims are likely to be regarded with suspicion unless you can support yourself compellingly. It's hard enough to get another job while you're still employed or in college, but still harder to do so when you're unemployed.

So how do you avoid being fired? It depends on the situation. In general, don't assume that you're performing satisfactorily just because your boss hasn't yelled at you. Most bosses don't yell. They have more subtle ways of showing displeasure. If you have gotten no positive feedback, whether oral or written, on your work, or if the feedback has been negative or nonexistent, you need to be concerned. Ask your boss for a short appointment to discuss some questions you have about your most recent assignments. You don't want to appear insecure or in need of hand holding, so be calm and confident. Explain that you want your work to be exceptionally good, and ask for tips on how you might improve your performance. Then follow your boss' advice carefully.

You should also try to identify a successful person at the company who has the same boss and job title as you—or maybe someone who used to have your job. Try to enlist that person's assistance. She will be able to give you the key to interpreting your boss's instructions, a list of pitfalls to avoid, and a clear idea of what is expected of you.

Unfair as it may seem, you may be fired for no good reason. Maybe you hit it off splendidly with the high-level manager who hired you, but the supervisor who you wound up reporting directly to resents the fact that he wasn't consulted about the decision to offer you a job. Or maybe he just doesn't like your looks. Whatever the reason, you don't have to be a willing victim. Pay attention to the vibes you get at work. If you're facing a lot of unwarranted hostility, brush up on those diplomacy skills and address the problem head-on before you wind up axed. Realize, however, that if your boss really has it in for you, your options are limited. You either work it out with him directly or resign yourself to a new job search. Going over his head will probably backfire. A manager's decision to fire an entry-level employee is unlikely to be questioned. The company has more invested in the manager than it does in you. If things aren't working out, you would be smart to heed the advance warning signals, pull out your list of contacts, and start work on Plan B.

You may also be let go because of downsizing. This, however, is not a reflection on your performance (unless you were the CEO). Your company may lay off dozens to hundreds of workers at a time when severe financial hardship strikes. If you lose your job for such a reason, you need not be embarrassed. Most likely, prospective employers will already know that your former company was in trouble. The layoff you were part of may even have been in the business press. Still, it's best not to be caught unaware if layoffs are looming. Luckily, graduating college seniors are currently finding plenty of employment in a strong economy. But the economy or the industry you work in may sour. No matter what your function is in your company, try to stay aware of its financial health and prospects for growth. If profits are plunging and top managers are scrambling, think about moving to a more secure company before you lose your job.

Results and Methods

Although you may sometimes doubt it, you can be pretty sure that your boss wants you to be promoted rather than fired. Your success will do him credit, while your failure will in part be seen as his own failure. In order to help you succeed, the boss can communicate with you in two important ways. It's of essential importance that you distinguish between these two kinds of communication.

One thing the boss can tell you is how results are measured, and what will be a bad, passable, or great result. An entirely different kind of communication he can deliver is to tell you how he proposes that you go about getting the results he wants—what methods he expects you to use. Second-guessing the boss about what results he needs is almost sure to be fruitless, if not counterproductive. However, his suggestions about methods need to be considered much more critically.

I was told to analyze ways to reprice our products in order to get more revenue. I thought it would make more sense to increase sales volume, but I didn't say so. I went ahead and came up with a much more effective set of price changes than the ones the boss had suggested that I analyze.

—*Andrea, age 26*

The result Andrea's boss wanted was to get more dollars from the same volume of product sales, by increasing prices. Andrea thought the company should aim at a quite different result, namely, an increase in sales volume without any increase in price. But she didn't argue with the objective the boss had set. To do so would have been inappropriate, and almost surely ineffective, because top management targets the overall performance levels and delegates the task of figuring out how to achieve them.

However, the boss' instructions didn't limit Andrea to considering only the kinds of price changes that he had specifically suggested. He himself may well have regarded those proposals as no more than examples of ideas to be evaluated. Obviously, when Andrea presented her analysis, she didn't say: "Here's your plan and my plan, and here's the proof that mine is better." She would have been wise to fudge the issue of what plan came from where. "After we talked, it opened my eyes to a lot of new possibilities, so I went further with the ideas you gave me."

Trying to get credit for originality and initiative is always problematic. You can attract envy and objections rather than praise. Don't insist on pointing out your successes all the time. Just get the good results, associate yourself with the good results, and the credit will take care of itself.

> Don't ever imagine that slavishly following the method the boss suggests is going to immunize you from blame if your work doesn't turn out well. It will not. You are responsible for the results. If the results are read as unsatisfactory, your compliance with advice and instructions will give you no shelter from criticism.

I was told to find the site for our new distribution center. I did it the way I was told, with the people I was told to use, but there were too many conflicting requirements and in the end the boss threw it out because he didn't like the costs.

—*Marilyn, age 27*

Marilyn probably could not have gotten the objectives changed, but she would have had a better chance of success if she had adapted to the difficulties facing her project and varied her methods accordingly. Almost any legitimate method is acceptable, if it gets you the required results. If you can find absolutely no way to satisfy the declared objectives, then you need to try to renegotiate them. Predicting bad results is unpleasant and harmful, but not nearly as bad as turning in unsatisfactory results when good ones were expected.

Building Up Your Contact Capital

When you start your first day of work, you will have something more to your credit than just a job. You will also have a network of contacts and acquaintances that can help you perform in that first job, and then find and perform in your second and subsequent jobs. Your contacts include professors, people you have worked with and to whom you have given help or from whom you have received help, and fellow students, or former fellow students.

If you're well organized, a substantial part of this capital is to be found in your personal telephone directory, Filofax, or Rolodex. This will include some addresses and some brief descriptive information. More likely, you carry a lot of the names and background in your head, refreshing this data as the need arises. These are the people you would hope to count on for the information and ideas that you need, as well as the linkage to still further sources, so that you won't be limited by your own individual experience in doing your job.

> *More and more of us have "knowledge" jobs. And when knowledge is the key resource, then you always need to have the right people to call, so that their knowledge can flow into yours. I do the same for them.*
>
> *—Peter, age 34*

Every day, your stock of contact capital is changing. If you are not adding to it and renewing it, then it is eroding and degrading. Telephone number and employer information becomes obsolete. You forget some of the people and they forget you. Hence you have to develop some additional contacts, and refresh aging ones, in order to maintain your effectiveness.

Some renewal of your contact capital comes about randomly and without any special initiative on your part, as people you have known contact you and come together with you at least verbally. But you need to do more than respond. You need to develop a process by which you maintain and interact with the whole of your contact file. One way to do this is to set a fixed part of the file to be worked every week. These people will receive a call or e-mail from you. The messages don't all have to be 100 percent different from each other, but they will be adapted somewhat to the recipient's position and interests. With practice, you will find that it requires very little effort to be interesting and—even better—to offer something valuable in each communication that you make.

> *I used my computer system to organize my contacts under key words, such as "sales management" and "Midwest." As my work moves along and I find I have something to give or to request, I check the people I have under the corresponding key word and I e-mail them.*

—*Doris, age 28*

Does Doris' system sound like a lot of work? It seemed that way to her at the beginning, but it became easier with practice, and she was increasingly motivated and justified by the benefits to her that it generated. The computer file supports and stimulates a system of recall and cross-connection that is increasingly internalized, speedy, and responsive.

A complementary or alternative system is based on a "tickler file." You assign a review data to each name based on a short interval for people who are likely to be important for you, and progressively longer periods for those who are more remote in their interests or in their relationship to you. When a name comes up, you make contact.

No one of these methods is likely to be ideal or sufficient for you. Your starting point has to be motivation and perceived need. These will push you towards more intense involvement and more active communication.

I used to resent all the time I spent on the phone. I know people who are so overwhelmed by their e-mail that they go off the system. The challenge I have surmounted is to make all these contacts work, for me and for them, rather than having them turn into useless work for all of us.

—Desmond, age 27

Communication in itself is a cost, not a source of value. The value created by the communication exceeds this cost only if you're multiplying talent and constructive involvement. It's not social, it's not routine, and it's very much dependent on deepening and enhancing your skills.

Think about the people you know who do the most, the people who can help you the most. These are very likely the people who have the most and the strongest contacts. When you ask them a question or for help, they pick up the phone or send a message. It seems natural and effortless, but it's not a reward for position or an indicator of personal charm. Rather, it's a habit pattern and a competence, a resource that naturally tends to expand as your horizon and accomplishments broaden.

Adding to your contact capital occurs at the individual level, but your capital also is enriched as you join and contribute to groups.

Talk to everyone you can. You'll find that you'll end up making some unexpected and potentially very useful contacts. I especially recommend attending industry association and club events. I made a great many useful contacts at events at the Advertising Club of New York and Adverstising Women in New York. Many of the associations and clubs offer junior memberships for a small fee.

—Abby Wittenberg, age 25

Individuals that she knew led Abby to groups and helped her to become affiliated with them. The groups, in turn, put her in touch with greatly expanded numbers of additional individuals. The point is not to go and have lunch or listen to a speech. That's not of much use in itself. The point is to pump oxygen into your contact network at an increasing pace and stimulate its expansion.

Others Will Define You

You will be dealing with many people who are not part of your personal network or team. When you start your job, you're little more than a colorless marker or pawn on the board. You are known to few in the organization, and most likely to none of the customers, vendors or people in other departments with whom you may need to deal. Furthermore, once you start work, no one is even going to ask for your résumé—much less actually read it. Think about that. They may be interested in getting your help, or working with you, but they won't give a hoot about your credentials. Why is that?

The reason people in your company, not to mention customers, contractors, or other new contacts, don't care about the document that was only recently so vitally important in establishing who you are is because they prefer to find this out for themselves—by interacting with you. They will give 100 percent weight to the evidence by provided by what you say and do with them, and 0 percent to such outdated measures as your GPA and even your internships. And if you start to get into trouble, there will be no use at all in saying: "No, I'm right! I'm obviously right. After all, I got a GPA of 4.0 at State!"

I've known a few people here who had been told so often that they were geniuses that they began to believe it themselves. But who are the big winners here, the ones who get promoted fast? Are they the guys who were top students and who have the highest IQs? Well, is our chairman the smartest man in the place? I don't think so.

—*Inez, age 33*

> The fact that you had brilliant accomplishments in five different internships loses its relevance once you're on the job. Your performance, not your potential, will now be the subject of evaluation. And you will be treated in the first instance according to your precise position in the organization, rather than according to who you are as an individual.

This is a humbling fact, full of promise but also full of risk. Once your job begins, you're going to be defining yourself to others. You won't do it by answering questions on "my most challenging experience." You won't do it by making claims of competence and interest. No, you will do it by the way you carry out your job. And in doing your job, you will be writing on a blank slate.

If you don't keep your promises, then customers and coworkers will hate you no matter what GPA you compiled or how many teams you captained. Maybe you got away with it at school, or at home, but not on the job. If you waste people's time with idle chatter, self-promotion, or flattery, then the more worthwhile of them will quietly avoid you. If you're indifferent to people, then you will become invisible and transparent to them, a blank. If you are careless or biased in your judgments, if your reasoning is unsound or confused, the word will get around and you will be shunned.

After a few weeks, a manager from another department came in and said he was interested in having me work on a project. He gave me a two-page memo and asked for my reactions. After I gave it, he walked out without a word. I guess he didn't like my answer.

—Thomas, age 25

Welcome to the real world. You're going to be judged on what you do—on how well you think and express yourself, and on the relevance and effectiveness of your actions, on your results. It's as if everything you say or write goes into a tape recorder and is available for all to hear. Unlike a résumé or interview, you don't have the privilege of creaming off the sweetest moments and forgetting everything else. This is going to make you look quite different.

So, on day one of your job, you must revise your self image in order to be able to see yourself as others see you. Drop all the baggage, and particularly the pride and self importance that enlarged you on campus, at least as a graduating senior on the top rung of the ladder. Every time you act on the job, ask yourself how your actions characterize and rate you. Are you making excuses? Are you marking yourself as mediocre and unambitious? Or are you committing to the best and doing the best? Are you showing insight and initiative, or merely being ornery and negative?

They had us do an exercise here: rate ourselves and rate each other on characteristics such as articulateness and problem-solving ability. Amazing! No insight at all. We just weren't seeing ourselves as others saw us.

—Patricia, age 26

The actions you take, and the ways in which people react to them, won't be always the same in quality, but they certainly won't be random. You will build a reputation, an image, and a place for yourself. Your reputation may not be entirely accurate, and it certainly won't be exactly what you want. But you will have the opportunity to improve and update it.

If you think about people you have known at work and even before, you will see that many seemed oblivious to the impressions they created, and willfully ignorant of their reputations and of the expectations that others had of them. This is a pitfall that you must escape, in part by becoming a more sensitive observer and in part by developing relationships that encourage candor and confidence. Your progress will be determined by how you are perceived by others, and you can't influence these perceptions positively and efficiently unless you know and understand them.

There's a continuity and intensity in work relationships that you may not have encountered before, except with your family or with a roommate or best friend. Your family and friends, though, had strong personal reasons to be tolerant and optimistic when dealing with you. Your boss and your coworkers can't afford to be tolerant of your mistakes, because their own work will be imperiled by them. They can't afford to be overly optimistic about your performance, because you may drag them down with you.

Every now and again I see someone who is dangerous. Bad judgment, lack of insight, slipshod thinking, overoptimism. All I can do is informally try to sidetrack those people to assignments where they'll do less harm.

—Peggy, age 44

Make sure you're the kind of coworker and employee that people won't want to sidetrack or avoid.

Circumventing the Weaknesses of Others

At work, interdependence is even more widespread than teamwork. You will sense who is a strong contributor and who is merely getting by for the moment. As an entry-level recruit, you're unlikely to be able to either motivate or teach people enough to turn them from detriments to assets. You're more likely to succeed by working around weak people, rather than by working through them. This can be done be redefining tasks, by shouldering more of the burden yourself, and by finding other resources that are more effective.

> *When I needed an advertising letter, the Marketing Services Department would give me a weak one, and then argue. I learned how to write the letters myself. That learning was actually one of the most valuable things I got out of the job.*
>
> *—Kathryn, age 26*

Learning to do someone else's job rather than relying on "experts" is valuable both in the short and long run. Kathryn did more than gain confidence in herself as an advertising copywriter:

> We had a lawyer who was a real pussyfooter. He always wanted to weaken the letters. I politely took these problems up the line in the legal department. I learned how to cite regulations and precedents. I developed positive relationships with more senior lawyers.
>
> *—Kathryn, age 26*

Functional experts, whether they are copywriters or lawyers, are supposed to serve as resources rather than obstacles. But some of them are not equipped to do their jobs well, either because they lack necessary skills or because they are not motivated to face towards your business objectives. Some feel that their mission is to act as a check on you rather than to help you. When you run into such a situation, your best recourse is to learn to do some of the functional tasks better than the experts can do them.

It's sometimes said that you deserve to be a boss only if you can do the job of each person reporting to you better than that person can do it. That is an exaggeration. However, you won't get far as a home builder if you're ignorant of plumbing and electricity and you rely on the "experts" to tell you what can and should be done in these specialties. Likewise, you won't get far as a marketer if you can't personally add a lot of value to your marketing communications and resolve legal issues in a heads-up, goal-oriented manner.

Mentoring

In the college setting, a mentor can help steer you towards your goals. If you have a mentor who is well connected with employers, he can help you obtain job offers. Because the college setting is generally far less intense than the workplace setting, there's seldom much risk of a conflict between mentor relationships or between a mentor relationship and your relationships with friends and fellow students. Colleges expect their professors and other administrators to take an interest in individual students, so mentoring is generally viewed in a positive light.

My mentor was the executive vice president of the university and he lived in my residence hall. He helped me tremendously in my decision as to whether to go to law school or work. If you can, I would recommend getting mentors in different areas—a past employer, friends who have recently graduated, your parents and their friends, and professors or administrators at your university.

—Thomas, age 29

At work, the context and the possibilities are quite different. While a few employers, such as law and consulting firms, make formal provision for mentoring and officially encourage it, most organizations don't. You're on your own. If a senior person other than your immediate boss takes a visible interest in your career, this will almost surely arouse jealousy on the part of coworkers. Even having lunch in the cafeteria or meeting in the office with a person who is not directly involved with your work can generate curiosity.

The underlying issue is favoritism. A college mentor probably won't be in a position to raise your grades or get you a scholarship. However, a mentor on the job might be instrumental in getting you a raise or a promotion. In fact, the influence of a mentor can gravitate into a wide range of informal communications that can lead to someone offering you a better position. Since most people are not advancing or being rewarded as quickly as they would like, some see themselves as victims of arbitrariness and favoritism. Sometimes this is detached from any concern about one-on-one mentoring relationships.

Around here, they either like you or they don't. If they do, you get ahead no matter how much you screw up. If they don't—there's no sense in even trying.

—Pete, age 28

Inadequately designed or implemented human resources systems, poor downward communication and undisciplined management practices fan the flames of resentment. *Favoritism* means treating employees differently from each other, in ways that don't reflect actual or reasonably anticipated accomplishment. In an important sense, mentoring is almost inevitably a form of favoritism, because the mentor relationship is not earned entirely or even primarily on the basis of merit. Rather, it's based at least in part on natural affinity, often arising from shared experiences or interests. Having gone to the same college is one of these.

Here is an interesting example:

> *The people I met at Brown have been the most valuable thing I've gotten out of my college experience. At The Motley Fool, an Internet startup I cofounded, the CFO and COO are both Brown grads.*
>
> —*Tom Gardner, cofounder, The Motley Fool*

Now, if you worked there and you didn't go to Brown, you might feel that you were at a disadvantage—even though you were treated entirely fairly. If you observed one or more mentor relationships between Brown alumni, you might be prone to grumble about favoritism, even though the common bond felt by the Brown alumni was not directed against you and deprived you of no advantages.

In this situation, grumbling or feeling disadvantaged will do you no good at all. Better to develop some knowledge and some positive feelings about the Brown experience and the Brown contingent. Take advantage of the fact that if one of them likes you, others will be inclined to agree.

> At work, as at college, only a small percentage of people have any significant mentor relationship. In both places, this reflects both shyness and lack of initiative. Mentor relationships are nonexclusive. You should pursue every opportunity to develop them, because the benefits far outweigh any potential drawbacks. The benefits include advice, information, and access to opportunities both inside the organization and beyond.

To acquire a mentor or mentors, the first requirement is simple receptivity. After you're hired, make sure to recontact and thank each of the people in the organization who interviewed you. Be on the alert for any invitation to "come back and tell me how you're doing." Express interest in their jobs, and about anything else in their lives that they have told you about.

I had three rounds of interviews and met a total of eight people. I don't work with any of them directly, but three of them I continue to see regularly. They take a kindly interest and they want to help me.

—Martin, age 25

When I interviewed, a number of the older people with small children were very interested in the fact that I had gone through bilingual education. They wanted some comments and suggestions for their children. It was a great way to make friends in the company.

—Abe, age 23

It makes no difference whether the word *mentor* has ever been uttered between Martin and any of these three more senior people, or whether he has ever spoken or even thought of them under that label. Martin has gained the advantages of mentoring by seizing the first opportunities available. At the beginning, be intensive rather than selective in maintaining and intensifying contact with those you meet.

You may occasionally feel shocked, or at least surprised, when someone asks a question about your work or praises it. Follow up! Send additional material, ask for comments. That is how you fan the spark.

My boss brought me along to a big meeting, and I was asked to comment briefly on a couple of data issues. As people filed out of the room, two managers I didn't know came over. One wanted more information and the other said she appreciated what I had to say.

—Marie, age 24

Those two contacts were big potential opportunities. At a minimum, each is a person who might think about offering Marie another, better job. Either or both might want to talk to Marie further, and this could lead to a mentoring relationship. Learn how to keep a conversation going in such a situation, rather than just saying "Yes," or "Thank you."

Even if the first spark doesn't immediately ignite a fire, make sure to keep it glowing. Stay in touch.

I had met a manager at a training session, and he seemed to notice me, though we chatted only briefly. A couple of months later he was promoted and I called to congratulate him. He invited me to lunch!

—Charles, age 30

Almost everyone has a profound fear of being seen as a "brownnoser." But if you're concise, sensitive, and sincere, then you're not a brown-noser. Friendliness and a positive attitude towards others, whatever their level in the organization, are qualities that are needed and appreciated everywhere, and they are rare. You can start with the receptionists and assistants, who can give you a great deal of help.

Within a year, you will also begin to have opportunities to act as mentor for less experienced associates. Seize those opportunities. They can bring you satisfaction and more than that, they can begin to build an infrastructure of people whose qualities and capabilities you know you can rely upon. You will need these people more than they need you when you're promoted or transferred and begin to take on organization-building responsibilities.

Afterword

Work, like college, will offer you many rewards, including the pleasure of learning and of collaborating with others. Thinking about what you want to accomplish and how to achieve it's a valuable habit to develop. Think about the results that you seek from your effort.

At college you need to know about how you will be graded, and at work you need to foresee how your boss will respond to what you do. You also need to make many choices in which current enjoyment or rewards have to be weighed against later ones. The decisions don't need to be laborious or painful, they need to be consistent and conscious.

Many people find themselves happier at work than they ever were in school.

> *I groove on creating value and becoming more valuable. At school I learned to enjoy learning, but I feel like the learning accelerated when I left school and went to work.*
>
> —Harvey, age 24

I hope that this book is of help to you in navigating through college into a fulfilling career.

Notes

Notes

Notes

About

KAPLAN

Educational Centers

Kaplan Educational Centers is one of the nation's premier education companies, providing individuals with a full range of resources to achieve their educational and career goals. Kaplan, celebrating its 60th anniversary, is a wholly-owned subsidiary of The Washington Post Company.

TEST PREPARATION & ADMISSIONS

Kaplan's nationally-recognized test prep courses cover more than 20 standardized tests, including entrance exams for secondary school, college, and graduate school as well as foreign language and professional licensing exams. In addition, Kaplan offers private tutoring and comprehensive, one-to-one admissions and application advice for students applying to graduate school.

SCORE! EDUCATIONAL CENTERS

SCORE! after-school learning centers help students in grades K-8 build academic skills, confidence, and goal-setting skills in a motivating, sports-oriented environment. Kids use a cutting-edge, interactive curriculum that continually assesses and adapts to their academic needs and learning style. Enthusiastic Academic Coaches serve as positive role models, creating a high-energy atmosphere where learning is exciting and fun for kids. With nearly 40 centers today, SCORE! continues to open new centers nationwide.

KAPLAN LEARNING SERVICES

Kaplan Learning Services provides customized assessment, education, and training programs to K-12 schools, universities, and businesses to help students and employees reach their educational and career goals.

KAPLAN INTERNATIONAL

Kaplan serves international students and professionals in the U.S. through Access America, a series of intensive English language programs, and LCP International Institute, a leading provider of intensive English language programs at on-campus centers in California, Washington, and New York. Kaplan and LCP offer specialized services to sponsors including placement at top American universities, fellowship management, academic monitoring and reporting, and financial administration.

KAPLOAN

Students can get key information and advice about educational loans for college and graduate school through **KapLoan** (Kaplan Student Loan Information Program). Through an affiliation with one of the nation's largest student loan providers, **KapLoan** helps direct students and their families through the often bewildering financial aid process.

KAPLAN PUBLISHING

Kaplan Books, a joint imprint with Simon & Schuster, publishes books in test preparation, admissions, education, career development and life skills; Kaplan and *Newsweek* jointly publish the highly successful guides, **How to Get Into College** and **How to Choose a Career & Graduate School**. *SCORE!* and *Newsweek* have teamed up to publish **How to Help Your Child Suceed in School**.

Kaplan InterActive delivers award-winning, high quality educational products and services including Kaplan's best-selling **Higher Score** test-prep software and sites on the internet (**http://www.kaplan.com**) and America Online. Kaplan and Cendant Software are jointly developing, marketing and distributing educational software for the kindergarten through twelfth grade retail and school markets.

KAPLAN CAREER SERVICES

Kaplan helps students and graduates find jobs through Kaplan Career Services, the leading provider of career fairs in North America. The division includes **Crimson & Brown Associates**, the nation's leading diversity recruiting and publishing firm, and **The Lendman Group and Career Expo**, both of which help clients identify highly sought-after technical personnel and sales and marketing professionals.

COMMUNITY OUTREACH

Kaplan provides educational resources to thousands of financially disadvantaged students annually, working closely with educational institutions, not-for-profit groups, government agencies and other grass roots organizations on a variety of national and local support programs. Also, Kaplan centers enrich local communities by employing high school, college and graduate students, creating valuable work experiences for vast numbers of young people each year.

KAPLAN

Want more information about our services, products, or the nearest Kaplan center?

1 Call our nationwide toll-free numbers:

1-800-KAP-TEST for information on our live courses, private tutoring and admissions consulting
1-800-KAP-ITEM for information on our products
1-888-KAP-LOAN* for information on student loans

2 Connect with us in cyberspace:

On AOL, keyword:"Kaplan"
On the World Wide Web, go to: http://www.kaplan.com
Via e-mail: info@kaplan.com

3 Write to:

Kaplan Educational Centers
888 Seventh Avenue
New York, NY 10106